MANAGING EMPLOYEE HONESTY

MANAGING EMPLOYEE HONESTY

BY CHARLES R. CARSON

Security World Publishing Co., Inc.
Los Angeles, Calif. 90034

First Edition 1977
Second Printing 1979

Security World Publishing Co., Inc.
2639 South La Cienega Boulevard
Los Angeles, California 90034

Printed in the United States of America

Library of Congress Cataloging in Publication Data

Carson, Charles R   1905-
  Managing employee honesty.

  Includes index.
  1. Employee theft. 2. Personnel management.
3. Industry — Security measures. I. Title.
HF5549.5.E43C37   658.4'7   76-51836
ISBN 0-913708-27-5

Contents

Section I

HONESTY AS A CONTROLLABLE VARIABLE

Chapter 1

The Relativity of Honesty

Before meaningful discussion is possible of any subject that begins with an abstraction, such as honesty, we need first to be sure that we are all talking about the same thing.

What is honesty? How would you define it? Unfortunately, there can be almost as many meanings as there are people, because most people tend to slant their definitions to excuse some of their own small dishonesties. However, most of us would accept the general sense of the term given in Webster's Unabridged Dictionary, where honesty is defined as "fairness and straightforwardness of conduct, speech, etc.; integrity; truthfulness; freedom from fraud."

In the context of a book on employee honesty, those concepts of fairness, straightforwardness and integrity acquire particular application to the employee-employer relationship. For our purposes, then, honesty can be defined as *respect for the rights and property of others*. It is that quality which makes a person (employee) trustworthy, truthful and law-abiding.

No one, it should be said, completely fulfills this ideal; rather, people are "relatively honest." Each of us, including the author, has a variable degree of honesty that is less than total.

If it is to be effective, therefore, security must be based on a controlled degree of relative honesty. Punishing employees caught stealing will not, by itself, reinforce relative honesty or control dishonesty. A security system that tries only to identify past thieves adds its own costs to losses already sustained, it never catches all the employees who have stolen, and it does nothing to prevent future thefts.

This concept of security's role in keeping employees honest is based upon four fundamental truths, which might here be termed "Carson's Laws." These are:

1. No one is completely honest.
2. Honesty is a variable that can be influenced for better or worse.
3. Temptation is the father of dishonesty.
4. Greed, not need, triggers temptation.

Recognizing these basic realities, a good security system must start with relatively honest employees working under a plan to prevent them from being tempted into dishonesty. The employer must assume a moral responsibility not to tempt employees to steal.

Relative Dishonesty

Those who are challenged by the statement that no one is completely honest are quick to retort, "Are you calling *me* dishonest?" However, a little self-examination will lead the most upright reader to discover small dishonesties in his own actions, and to recognize the same small dishonesties in people around him.

For example, as the driver of an automobile, did you ever

• Drive faster than the posted speed limit?
• Stay in a metered parking space beyond the time you paid for?

Because these are such small violations, we do not consider them criminal acts until the rare instance when we are caught. Even then we tend to dismiss them as bad luck rather than dishonest acts. The next time you get caught violating a traffic law, listen to yourself as you grumble, "Police have time to catch me driving 30 miles an hour in a 20-mile school zone, but they don't have time to catch holdup men." Or, "They never seem to ticket cars parked illegally in front of my place of business."

Frivolous examples? Let us go up the scale of dishonesty:

- If an error is made in your favor in computing the price of something you buy, do you report it?
- If a cashier gives you too much change, do you return it?
- When was the last time you made out a completely honest tax return?
- If you travel on an expense account, how often have you turned in a completely honest accounting?
- If you found a purse containing money and the owner's identification, would you return the money to the owner if the amount was $10? $100? $1,000?

As we proceed step by step into greater dishonesty, at some point, early or late, each of us reaches our limit of honesty. That point marks our degree of relative honesty.

Complete honesty does not exist; honesty is a variable.

Two Types of Honesty

As a person reaches employable age, relative honesty is the sum of two types of honesty, *moral* and *conditioned*. Moral honesty is instilled in us during formative childhood years. It is religion. It is conscience. It is the subconscious compulsion to do things honestly. Moral honesty needs no prompting.

This kind of honesty develops largely from early childhood influences: the pain of being spanked, the mental anguish of being denied a favorite toy, the stern face and forceful voice of a correcting parent. Moral honesty comes from seeing others rewarded for kindness, or from attempting to live up to the heroic image of a respected older person. This type of experience affects a child before he has full reasoning capacity, and it reflects the relative honesty of adults around him.

Conditioned honesty, as opposed to moral honesty, is the result of reasoned fear of the consequences of being caught in a dishonest act. This induced honesty comes from conscious thought, and it requires an intelligent reasoning capacity. If that reasoning is good, a person will not engage in a dishonest act when the chance of getting caught seems to outweigh the benefits of the misdeed. This conditioning is the result of experience and fear.

Even if a person's reasoning is not good and he is caught in a dishonest act, he can still be conditioned toward later honesty. Exposure, punishment and reduced earning power are among the conditioning influences.

Good reasoning that leads to a decision against a dishonest act carries its own reward. No one else knows that the individual considered acting dishonestly; hence, he acquires no stigma. After someone has been caught in a dishonest act, on the other hand, the memory of his dishonesty can never be wiped out of the minds of others. They will remember that he was dishonest long after they have forgotten the details of his act. But the stigma of dishonesty may also condition the individual to a higher level of honesty in order to demonstrate to others that he has "learned his lesson."

People with little moral honesty and poor reasoning power may be beyond conditioning. These are the repeating criminal offenders who make the same mistakes over and over.

How much of your honesty is moral and how much conditioned? You are the best judge, and there is a simple way to grade yourself. If an honest action comes without a conscious decision, it stems from moral honesty; if you stop to look over your shoulder, so to speak, conditioned honesty has entered the picture.

Honesty Is Conditioned by Positive Security

While each of us starts adult life with varying degrees of moral and conditioned honesty, the controllable factor in our total honesty is that of conditioning. The most important function of a security system, therefore, is to condition employees toward greater honesty.

If there is little or no system to prevent dishonesty, employees who are easily tempted will start to steal. The more honest employees will resist temptation longer, but the knowledge that others are successfully stealing will ultimately induce some of them to steal. Constant temptation will erode their moral honesty.

When an employee's moral honesty has been lowered by temptation, there is no evidence until he is caught stealing. Security failed much earlier, however — not when the theft became known, but when the employee was first tempted to steal. A good security system removes temptations, or makes the temptations appear dangerous or unprofitable through conditioning. Security succeeds when positive conditioning reinforces moral honesty to induce greater honesty.

A positive security system must exert pressures constantly to induce this higher degree of employee honesty, and the system must change with changing conditions. Employees come and go, plant organization and manufacturing processes change. Security must also adapt.

Management cannot set exact standards of honesty for all jobs. Nor can one person tell all managers what degree of honesty should be required. Degrees of temptation vary from job to job; accordingly, the degree of honesty demanded of employees will also vary. Management should use this criterion: *the job should not tempt an employee into dishonesty.* Because honesty is a variable that is constantly under pressure to change, management should ensure that the employee's initial quotient of honesty will not be eroded by the extent of temptation on the job. The security system should then motivate employees toward greater honesty.

More Temptation, More Theft

Changes in the level of moral honesty from generation to generation result from changes in those influences that build character. The enormous increase in all types of crimes in recent years strongly suggests that these formative influences have weakened. Their decline has placed added responsibility on business managers and their security systems to reduce the opportunity and temptation to steal.

Since personal experience is sharper and more detailed than that reported by others, the author must turn to his own formative years for comparison with the present. He was raised in a small Midwestern town. He had few possessions that anyone would want to steal. Family friends and neighbors had few tempting possessions; houses were never locked. There were always relatives and friends who saw or heard about everything that happened in town. Everyone knew that he could not enjoy anything he was tempted to steal. In this environment, a lack of temptation and a fear of sure detection were strong factors in developing moral honesty in youngsters and conditioning toward greater honesty when they became adults.

This small town influence has steadily decreased during the past half century. Modern retail practices have placed us within driving distance of large shopping centers where both shopper and shopkeeper are anonymous. The stores are largely self-service. Increased accessibility of merchandise increases the temptation to steal and leads to increased thefts. And the observant relatives and neighbors who were once a strong local deterrent are no longer present to counter the temptation.

In short, those influences that build moral and conditioned honesty are decreasing; the restraints of the past are gone. Today's higher crime rates reflect this combination of increased temptation and lessened surveillance.

Crime Statistics Mirror Change

Uniform Crime Reports have been compiled nationally by the Federal Bureau of Investigation since 1930; the first complete year for which statistics were collected was 1931. The FBI divides crimes into various categories for comparative purposes. "Larceny-Theft" is the category that perhaps most closely reflects the honesty of the general population. The FBI describes Larceny-Theft as "the unlawful taking or stealing of property or articles of value without the use of force or violence or fraud." This category does not include confidence schemes or auto thefts.

For 1931, a Depression year, the FBI figures from 73 cities with over 100,000 population showed a total of 165,630 larceny-theft reports. The 1935 total from the same cities was 179,102; the 1938 figure, 193,788. The eight-year increase was about 14.5%, which just matched the increase in working population for the same period. The rate of this crime in relation to population, therefore, did not increase during this period.

In 1938 the average number of such reported crimes per 100,000 population for thirty-six cities with over 250,000 population was 927.9. The total per 100,000 population in 1,120 cities under 10,000 population was only 480.1, or just over half. The small town influence against dishonesty was still being felt in 1938.

By 1944 the war years had distorted many things, so that apt comparisons could not be made with pre-war statistics. There was a 13.3% decrease in the rate of Larceny-Theft overall. The rate in cities under 10,000 population was still about half the rate for the entire country.

The following chart compares the rates of reported Larceny-Theft crimes in smaller and larger cities over a 20-year period. The percentages record the amount of increase over the prior year listed (e.g., the 1964 figure for larger cities was 82% higher than the 1954 figure).

Reported Larceny-Theft Crimes Per 100,000 Population

Year	Cities Over 250,000 Pop.	Percent Increase	Cities Under 10,000 Pop.	Percent Increase
1954	1,088.2		671.4	
1964	1,984.2	82	922.9	37
1969	2,819.3	42	1,520.2	65
1974	3,171.4	12	2,406.3	58

This chart indicates that Larceny-Theft crimes have increased faster in the smaller cities than in the larger. If this trend continues, the rates per 100,000 population will soon be the same in large cities and small. The family-community deterrent to dishonesty seems no longer to exist.

The following excerpt from the 1974 Uniform Crime Reports, based on statistics from a broader base than the above chart, confirms this conclusion:

"During 1974, the larceny crime rate was 2,473 offenses per 100,000 inhabitants, an increase of 20% from the 1973 rate. The rate has increased 29% since 1969. In 1974, the larceny rate in the metropolitan areas was 2,831 per 100,000 inhabitants, 808 in the rural areas, and 2,543 per 100,000 inhabitants in cities outside any metropolitan areas."

Establishing Deterrents

If a security system is to reduce employee theft, the effect of former deterrents to dishonesty must be re-established. Security measures must condition employees to honesty. Further dishonesty cannot be controlled by acting only after it is discovered. It must be attacked where it starts; it cannot be swept under the rug.

Example: A costume jewelry manufacturer was faced with steady losses of gold wire used as raw material. Losses were high enough to threaten the solvency of the business. Employees were told that continued losses were threatening their jobs.

All employees were asked to take lie detector tests, but were promised that no one would lose his job unless the tests showed major thefts. The polygraph tests did not discover any large thefts, but they did reveal that 94% of the employees were taking small quantities of wire for use at home or for family gifts. The remaining 6% had taken no wire.

When this 6% group was identified, it was found that they worked in the office or in other areas with no access to the gold wire stock. In all probability, the relative honesty of this group was no greater than that of the others; the test did not cover losses of items to which this group did have access, such as office supplies.

The jewelry company employees were told that lie detector tests would be given once a year to employees chosen at random and that any thefts disclosed would be cause for termination. The company also revised its application form to require the applicant to agree to polygraph tests as a condition of employment and as a basis for job termination.

Employees were conditioned toward a higher level of honesty, and losses were reduced.

Example: A main-street department store hired a private investigator to determine the cause of steady, regular merchandise losses. The store's protection against shoplifters was good enough to rule out large losses from that cause. Certain main floor departments were having the greatest losses; all of the clerks involved were women. A female undercover investigator was hired as a clerk at the first vacancy on the first floor. She was hired through regular procedures and went through the training that all new clerks were given.

Meanwhile, a study was made of a variety of ways in which employees could get merchandise out of the store. While this study was being made, the undercover clerk overheard a fellow employee borrow lunch money from another clerk because she had forgotten her purse that morning. When the forgetful clerk left the store that night, however, the undercover clerk noticed that she had a purse with her. It was identical to several other purses on the sales counter.

The next day the investigator took a look at the purses carried to work by the other clerks. About half of them were identifiable as having come from the store's stock. All clerks could buy store merchandise at a substantial discount if the purchase was approved by a supervisor, but the floor supervisor could not remember ever approving an employee's sales slip for a purse.

Subsequently, costume jewelry worn by many clerks was identified as store merchandise; again, there were no recorded sales slips approved by the supervisor. Clerks were then seen openly taking handkerchiefs and cosmetics off the store counter for their own use. The clerks were filling their personal needs out of the store's stock and paying for nothing.

There was no security plan to prevent employee thefts. Employees could even carry packages out at night without any approval or inspection. The security personnel were always on the first floor looking for shoplifters but never seemed to see employees stealing merchandise. Possibly the security employees were also helping themselves to the store's merchandise. The clerks were stealing from each other's departments so openly that all clerks must have had at least a guilty knowledge of the thefts.

The investigator made many recommendations to the store management for procedures to reduce temptation and condition employees toward greater honesty. Management refused to follow any of these suggestions for fear of hurting the feelings of the employees, many of whom had been with the store ten years or more. Six months later the store went out of business, unable to make enough profit to stay solvent. Because it was unwilling to remove temptation or to condition its employees toward honesty, the store bled to death from general internal dishonesty.

Material losses are always high in poorly protected areas. Where there is little security, employees will be dishonest. To condition employees to greater honesty, management must remove temptation and provide constant security surveillance. And not only must that conditioning toward honesty be constant; it must also be visible. It must make its presence known to the employees.

Chapter 2

Contributing Factors in Employee Theft

There are no completely accurate statistics available on employee dishonesty. Employers are always reluctant to discuss or report employee dishonesty; they seldom report it to police authorities. FBI crime reports, however, do show a steady yearly increase in general dishonesty levels, and employees, of course, are drawn from this general group.

Statistics from surety bond companies provide data only on those companies covered by surety bonds where losses are reported. Many losses are never reported because the employer finds himself paying back in higher premiums most of what he receives in claims. Many other losses are not reported for personal reasons; the employer absorbs the loss rather than injure the dishonest employee's reputation.

The following figures, based on surety bond losses, are the best available but probably reflect a higher degree of relative honesty than actually exists. These reports show that

- About 25% of bonded employees have a high degree of relative honesty. If one of them found a purse containing money and the owner's identification, the owner would stand a good chance of getting back the purse and money.
- Another 25% are so dishonest that they actively look for something to steal.

13

- The remaining 50% are only as honest as circumstances require; if one of this group were to find a purse, he would first consider the chances of getting caught if he kept the money. Only the conditioning influence of possible punishment keeps this group relatively honest.

This means that at best only 75% of the work force has enough moral and conditioned honesty to make acceptable applicants for employment. As a guideline for minimum applicant background investigation, the employer should determine if the applicant is one of the 25% actively looking for something to steal. (Standards for background investigations are discussed in more detail in Chapter 8.)

Why Employees Steal

What tempts relatively honest employees to steal? We are not talking about professional criminals or people with mental problems, but people who are fully employable and have no abnormal compulsions.

Employees caught stealing will usually claim financial need as their motive. Most cases, however, indicate that these people confuse need with greed. Their "need" is a desire for improved status, recognition or bolstered ego.

During the Depression of the 1930s, many people were under great pressure to provide their families with a bare existence. Yet crime reports for that period show a rate that is almost unbelievably low when compared with today's crime rates. Need alone causes few thefts. Desire for status and recognition, on the other hand, can be corrupting.

Stealing for Status

Example: Several members of a neighborhood church complained that they had not received credit for some envelope contributions made during Sunday services. The minister himself could not escape suspicion. Each Sunday's collection was put in an unlocked drawer of his study desk. This drawer was closed and locked after the collection was placed in it. The minister usually tallied and posted the contributions by himself and deposited the money in the bank. He was willing to pay for an investigation to clear himself. He did not want to prove any church member dishonest, but when a large contributor threatened to leave the church if the thefts did not stop, the minister sought a private investigator.

The minister's study was the most likely place for the thefts to take place. The collection plates were in full view of the church members until they reached the study door. A trap door in the study gave access to an attic above. An investigator in the attic had a good view of the desk area and the study door through a hole at the edge of a light fixture.

The investigator assumed his position in the attic before church services the next Sunday. He observed the man who brought in the collection plates looking through the envelopes in the plates. He took one envelope and placed it in his coat pocket. He put the rest of the plates' contents into the desk drawer and closed it. He than checked the drawer to make sure it was locked.

The same man regularly took the collection plates from the altar to the study each Sunday. He was a staunch church worker and highly respected by the congregation. It was considered necessary, therefore, to have another member of the church observe him in the act of theft. The minister did not want to be the one to do this.

A buzzer system was installed so that when the investigator in the attic pushed a button, a buzzer sounded in the pulpit. The minister asked a trusted officer of the church to help catch the thief.

The following Sunday, the investigator again observed the suspected thief remove an envelope from the plate and place it in his coat pocket. The investigator sounded the buzzer, and the minister signaled the trusted officer, who went to the study before the suspect had left the room. The desk drawer had been closed and locked. The suspect denied taking the envelope until the investigator opened the trap door and dropped into the study. The accused church member then produced the envelope and admitted taking one envelope each week for the past several months. He told of having volunteered a few times to help the minister record the envelope contributions so he could see which ones always contained currency. He denied ever using any of the money for himself; he always gave it to the church as his own contribution.

The minister was inclined to believe him. This member was always the first to contribute to any worthy cause or special church collection. He had become well-known in the congregation as the one person who could always be depended upon to start any collection. This set him above others in the congregation — and he was willing to steal to get that recognition.

Stealing to Cover Extra Expenses

Example. A woman clerk in a large department store had been discharged because her cash register drawer was short about $10 a day for several days a month. A private investigator was called in to prove the store's case against her after she filed suit asking for $100,000 damages. She could not get another job because the store refused to discuss her past employment with other companies where she applied for work.

The store had a system of cash registers with a drawer for each clerk. At the end of each work shift, each clerk counted out the amount of change assigned to her and placed it in an envelope, which she sealed and signed. She got this money back the next morning to use as change for the start of the new day. The clerk counted all the remaining money, sealed it in another envelope and gave it to the general cashier. The clerk had no way of knowing the total cash sales recorded in her register. The supervisor later opened the register and recorded totals for each clerk's sales for that day. The cash sale total would be compared by the cashier with the total recorded by the clerk on the second envelope.

Mechanically, it was a good system. However, there was no policing of employees' or supervisors' activities to ensure that they followed instructions in the use of the cash register.

When the clerk in question began to be short about $10 a day several times a month, this was such an unusual occurrence that management did not even tell her of any shortage except the first one. They assumed she had suddenly become a compulsive thief and watched her to obtain proof of their suspicions. All they proved was that she handled cash sales exactly according to store rules. Nevertheless, the shortages continued. The store discharged her and gave "personnel reduction" as the reason. The shortages stopped immediately; the store was sure she had been the thief.

The discharged clerk had been with the store for several years and knew the cash security system very well. It did not seem logical for her to continue to steal from her own cash drawer after being told of her first shortage. Other clerks in her section were interviewed for any information that would account for her losses, or any actions on her part that would indicate a change in her character. The only peculiarity noted was that she did not close her cash drawer after each sale. She was in the habit of pushing the cash drawer almost closed but not latching it as required by store regulations.

The clerk who replaced the suspected thief was closing and latching the drawer after each cash sale. The new clerk was instructed to leave the drawer unlatched as her predecessor had done. The second day on which she left the drawer unlatched, it was short $10.

An observation point was set up where all activity at that register could be watched secretly. The only unusual event observed was the floor supervisor unlocking and opening the inside register where the sales totals were shown. He did the same thing at two nearby registers. Normally these totals were not read until the clerks had counted their cash and left the sales area with the money sealed in envelopes. The supervisor did not record the register totals or make any use of the information from these unusual readings. There was no known reason for his action.

The replacement clerk was given a marked $10 bill and

instructed to keep it as the top bill in its cash drawer section and to report immediately if it disappeared. The next day the supervisor was again seen to check the inside totals on the same registers. A few minutes later, the clerk reported the marked bill was gone.

A store official stopped the supervisor nearby, took him to his office and asked him if he had taken any money from the register. Protesting his innocence, the supervisor produced what money he had in his pockets. The marked bill was there with his register keys. When the bill's markings were explained to him, he admitted taking it from the drawer.

As often happens in such cases, he at first admitted only what he knew could be proved. He said he unlocked the register cover and looked inside while leaning over the register. This covered the drawer while he inched it open and slipped the top $10 bill into his pocket. This was the only register he could steal from because it was the only one left open. He looked at the totals in some other nearby registers so he would not seem to be paying special attention to the one with the open drawer. When it was pointed out to him that the former clerk had also left her drawer open and had also suffered $10 losses, he admitted responsibility for those thefts as well.

The supervisor finally reached a point in his confession where he wanted to purge himself of all dishonest acts he had committed on the job. He admitted several isolated shortages where he had simply taken advantage of an opportunity of the moment. He also admitted responsibility for a series of unexplained central vault shortages. The vault cash had been short even packages of small bills a few times during the past two years, $100 to $500 at a time. There had been no pattern to these losses. It had been suspected that the armored car service or the bank could be responsible. The supervisor had been in a position to take this money when he was called to the vault area to verify shortages in clerks' sealed money envelopes.

Why did he begin to steal? It had all started about two years earlier when his daughter got married. He wanted to give her a large church wedding. The expenses got out of hand, and he stole from his employer. Unfortunately, he did not stop stealing when the wedding was paid for. He found other things on which to spend the extra money.

The recent cash register and vault shortages were solved. Further investigation showed that the supervisor had spent all the money he had taken; immediate recovery from him was unlikely. The store still faced the suit filed by the discharged clerk. They decided to offer to re-hire her.

Experience shows that employees are often tempted to steal to pay their bills ... but these bills are more likely to be for color TV sets or other luxury items than for groceries or medical services.

Moral Obligation of Management

The security department has the general responsibility of maintaining the relative honesty of all employees. Executives likewise have a special responsibility for the honesty of the people they supervise. (The particular problems of executive honesty will be covered in Chapter 8.)

Executives share the same influences of early moral training and later conditioning that affect their employees. Their promotions to executive positions usually indicate they have more experience, greater ability and better judgment than the average employee. Their judgement should enable them to see and avoid the temptations that lead to thefts. An executive should have a higher degree of total honesty than the average employee. He should be able to spot the temptations that might induce his employees to steal, and to isolate these temptations so they can be eliminated. This is his responsibility to his employees. The manner in which he assumes this responsibility is one measure of his executive ability.

Example. Several years ago, the U.S. Bureau of Narcotics and Dangerous Drugs seized about $300,000 in narcotics which had been purchased legally by an established drug wholesaler. The diversion of these drugs into illegal channels was the result of a lack of moral responsibility by management.

Undercover narcotic agents are always alert for new sources of drugs in illegal traffic. In this case they purchased narcotics from two men who had no legal right to sell them. Investigation showed that both men worked for the same wholesale drug company. Following their arrests, the government made an audit of the drug company's records of purchases and sales.

The audit showed a shortage of about 400,000 dosage units of narcotics and dangerous drugs. The report showed proper records of drug inventories were not being kept as required by federal law. Inventory records indicated that these shortages had been discovered earlier by management; they had attempted to cover up the losses by changing prices. A spokesman of the federal drug agency commented to a reporter: "Security provisions at the company's warehouse were lax and it was possible for persons to walk from the street into an area where soft drink machines were and simply take drugs off the shelf."

A stranger entering from the street to purchase a soft drink would have had to discover the availability of these drugs by accident. He would then have had to find out what trade name drugs could be sold in the illegal market. Company warehouse employees, on the other hand, knew the narcotics were there and that they had high illegal value. The company failed in its responsibility to control these dangerous substances. It failed its employees by making it too easy to steal these drugs.

The company's attempt to cover up its known losses was bad enough, but to take no action to prevent further losses amounted to criminal negligence. Its failure to protect its employees from temptation was a breakdown of moral responsibility. Management might have prevented two employees from being charged with serious criminal offenses.

In this case it is obvious that management caused the company to suffer serious financial loss. The company's executives failed in their corporate and personal responsibilities, and in failing to protect the honesty of employees, they failed a more important moral responsibility. Management falsified records to try to protect itself. It took no action to protect its employees.

Laxity of control is an open invitation to steal. Employees

will see the laxity and take advantage of it. This is conditioning toward dishonesty. While the drug firm's case is unusual in some ways, it illustrates a management attitude that is not unusual — acceptance of dishonesty as a silent partner in the business.

Businesses of all types are now absorbing theft losses by adding the cost of these losses to the sale prices of their products. They do not yet consider it immoral to treat dishonesty as a cost factor. The cost of sufficient security measures to control these thefts is also an acknowledged cost factor, but too often it is regarded as one to be avoided wherever possible.

Effects of Permitting Theft

In isolated instances, some attention is being given to the immorality of permitting thefts. These instances are so rare that they make news.

A few years ago the Associated Press distributed a story concerning shipping industry losses in the Port of New York running into millions of dollars each year. The Port Commissioners were reported as saying: "The shipping industry doesn't seem to care."

The commission set up two undercover stores to buy stolen cargo. They purchased stolen goods worth about $277,000. Of this total, only one bale of textiles (worth $940) had been reported stolen. The rest had been reported "short-landed" — that is, not received. Somewhere along the line back to the manufacturer, insurance paid for these losses. The insurance premium became part of the cost price. Insurance premiums increase as losses increase. The buying public is charged in turn for management's lack of interest in preventing losses.

The same news story also illustrated the direct moral cost of permitted thefts. Over a four-year period, the number of private pier guards arrested for stealing cargo exceeded the number of outside thieves apprehended for the same crime. If it is made easy for the guards to steal, can they be expected to protect property from other thieves?

The Port Commission charged the shipping industry with

reducing the number of guards, refusing to sign criminal complaints against known thieves, failing to provide adequate physical facilities to protect cargo, failing to report known theft losses, and not backing up those port watchmen who did perform their duties.

The results of management indifference to dishonesty are predictable. Employees will assume the same indifference, and temptation will induce employees to steal.

Participation of Management in Dishonesty

Where management recognizes employee dishonesty as a problem, it often cites cost as a bar to corrective action. Where management itself participates in dishonesty, it loses even this claimed justification for inaction.

Example: An investigator was called in several years ago to examine a case where a County Commissioner was suspected of taking bribes to influence his decisions on purchases. Each commissioner exercised some control over purchases of equipment used in his ward and had absolute freedom of action on emergency purchases.

Suspicion arose when this particular commissioner was taken unconscious to a hospital for emergency treatment. Among his belongings were found twelve new $100 bills. This man's poor financial condition was well known, and his possession of this much currency could not be explained from any known gainful employment. The story reached the County Prosecuting Attorney.

Investigation by the prosecutor pointed to the recent "emergency" purchase of a motorized road grader as a possible source of a kickback payment. The suspected commissioner had made this purchase although there was no real emergency need for it. No bids were called for and only one company was considered as a supplier. The total purchase price was about $25,000.

The company that sold the grader was a large authorized dealer for a well-known brand of heavy equipment. The district attorney asked for permission to review the company's records of this county purchase. The company agreed, and a private investigator was employed to search these records for evidence of a bribery payment.

By comparison with other sales, the investigator determined that the county had paid $5,000 too much for the road grader. This could have provided the money from which a bribe had been paid. It also established the probable size of the bribery payment, since the kickback is usually a little less than half the extra price paid.

In a kickback scheme, the buyer and seller usually agree to divide the increased price equally. The buyer does not verify the real price, so he does not know how much is added to it to establish the inflated selling price. Knowing this, the seller tells the buyer he is adding a little less than he really does add. In this way the seller always retains a little more than half the inflated amount. To him it is just good business.

The salesman who set up the road grader sale (and the kickback arrangement) made daily reports listing whom he called on and what he was trying to sell. One of these reports showed a call to the County Commissioner "about the money." On this date the seller wrote a check for $2,100 payable to "Cash." This was endorsed by the sales manager and cashed the same date. The bank paid it in $100 bills.

In the seller's accounting records this $2,100 was charged as an advance to the sales manager. He could not explain why the check was payable to "Cash," nor why he had cashed it instead of depositing it to his bank account.

With this and other evidence, the Prosecuting Attorney induced the salesman and the sales manager to testify for the prosecution. They stated that this check was the amount to be paid to the Commissioner as a kickback on the grader purchase. The payment was made in new $100 bills obtained when the check was cashed. The Commissioner was convicted of taking a bribe. Since the salesman and sales manager were needed as witnesses, they were not prosecuted for their roles.

The difference between the added $5,000 and the $2,100

paid as a bribe was retained by the selling company. It increased profits. To get this extra profit, the seller was willing to corrupt its own employees and a public official. Management participated actively in this illegal act.

Why did the seller let an outsider check records containing a kickback payment? Typically, the guilty company disguises the kickback transaction in its accounting records but usually forgets some other record. It feels secure if its accounting records do not reveal the transaction for what it was.

This type of one-time bribe or kickback usually involves sales to a city, county or some other political subdivision. Owners or managers of the selling companies are always involved in the schemes. The payment must start with a company check, which an official must sign. Someone with authority must decide how the charge is to be hidden in the accounting records. These are strictly management functions.

It is not unusual, however, to have these management dishonesties spawn lesser, but more continuous, employee dishonesties. The salesman starts to pad his gasoline and lunch purchases. Others involved find similar ways to augment their incomes. Management participation in dishonesty induces employee dishonesty. Employees are conditioned toward dishonesty.

Exposure and Prosecution

There is one common denominator in most cases of employee theft; that is, management's embarrassment over having employed a thief, over having been fooled, over suffering an unnecessary loss. This is the immediate feeling of the victim, whether a government agency, a bank or a commercial business. First questions are: Can publicity be avoided? Is it necessary to prosecute? Can we just discharge the thief and absorb our loss?

Too often this desire to save face rules the company's reaction to the theft. The dishonest employee is free to face the same temptations in his next job. The new employer is not warned that there are some jobs this employee should not be placed in until he proves his rehabilitation. In all fairness to the dishonest employee and his future employers, there should be some public record of his dishonesty.

If the employee seriously wants to reform, the stigma of dishonesty should be there to reinforce his desire. Without it he will face the next temptation with even less honesty. If the employee hides his past dishonesty in an employment application, normal diligence should make the record available to the new employer. This can only happen, however, if there *is* a record available.

Example. An FBI agent was once called in to investigate a shortage of about $200 at a bank. The loss was caused by a loan teller putting part of the collected loan interest payments in his own pocket. He had developed a bad habit of putting $5 to $10 into a pinball machine each day on his lunch hour, and he started "borrowing" some of the interest payments when his losses became too large for his salary. An internal auditor, on a routine audit, counted this teller's vault cash before the teller opened his cage for business. The cash was short about $200. The teller was charged in Federal court and received a short probationary sentence. He served no prison sentence, but his weakness was a matter of record for his succeeding employers.

The bank officers started searching for an experienced teller to replace the convicted thief. An experienced teller was located in a bank in a nearby city. With the recommendation of his employer, the new loan teller was hired.

Six months later the FBI agent was back to investigate another, much larger shortage in the cash of the new teller. The FBI made its usual background investigation in the city where he had previously been employed. (Such background investigations are made on first offenders to provide the court with the information it needs in determining proper sentence.)

One former fellow employee asked *which* shortage was being investigated. For the first time the FBI and the teller's new employer learned he had been short in his cash once before, at his former bank job. At that time he had been a paying teller whose cash had been short several hundred dollars. His father, a prominent businessman, paid off the shortage and influenced bank officials not to report the case to the FBI. Instead of being prosecuted, the dishonest teller was moved to the loan department where he handled only limited amounts of currency. He was recommended to the next bank looking for an experienced teller.

When this teller faced the court, he was a first offender as far as filed charges were concerned, but the judge knew of his prior dishonesty. As a result he was sentenced to a federal correctional institution. Had he been brought before the court on the actual first offense, he probably would have received a probationary sentence which would have required him to live an exemplary life for a specified length of time. This could have conditioned him toward greater honesty. The second dishonesty might have been prevented.

The first bank did him a disservice in not acting to condition him toward greater future honesty. It did the second bank a disservice in recommending him for the teller's job. The first bank violated the law (misprision of felony) in having knowledge of the commission of a felony and not reporting it to proper authorities. The first bank was not prosecuted for this violation, but after its attorneys explained the law and its penalties, the bank was well conditioned to report such matters in the future.

Conditioning is an important factor in changing an individual's total level of honesty. A known but unpunished or unpublicized act of dishonesty conditions toward further dishonesty. The need to remove the stigma of publicized dishonesty can condition toward greater honesty.

Management-Employee Relationship

As businesses grow in size or change ownership, the personal relationship between boss and employee practically disappears. Where there was once a very personal relationship, soon there is almost none.

Employees are isolated by the several layers of management

between them and executive power. The employees may have several levels of supervision above them. By the very nature of big business, various levels of management and supervision are also separated from one another. Employees do not consider themselves part of the company as a whole. Their feelings of togetherness seldom extend beyond their own work crew on their own shift.

To the employee, management in large corporations appears only as the paycheck. To management, the employee is a labor statistic. It is hard for either to picture the other in the personal terms that go with the words "trustworthy," "law-abiding," and "truthful." This is not said in criticism but as a fact that accompanies growth.

The larger the company, the more impersonal it naturally becomes. Management quits viewing its employees as individuals subject to an individual's temptations. The problems of employees become impersonal things to be handled during labor union negotiations. Management is then interested only in solutions, not in the problems, and their concern is further limited by the effect of those solutions on profits.

Conditioning employees toward greater honesty becomes more complex as the company becomes more complex. A competent security department is needed to prevent relative employee honesty from dropping as business complexity grows. The security department must keep pace with company expansion, and it must expand at the level of the average employee. Security cannot operate entirely at the executive level. Any expansion in size or to another location should always include an increase in the security staff. The relative honesty of employees must be managed and supervised in the same way competence and performance are supervised.

CASE HISTORY #1

J. Jones, a salesman traveling his territory in his own car, receives a travel allowance of 25¢ a mile from his company to pay all car expenses. The vehicle is also used as a second family car when he is at home. He considers the 25¢ a mile figure too low.

Jones reclaims this and other travel expenses in a monthly expense account. In this account he is required only to list a total of miles driven each day, with a total of miles for the month. He always claims total miles each month, business and personal, by making a small daily increase in mileage driven on company business. Around Christmas time his personal expenses are higher and his company car travel is less. His practice then is to add extra miles arbitrarily to his expense accounts for November and December.

The company pays expense accounts each month without auditing them. External auditors select a few salesmen each year for expense account audit. The salesmen know this because any errors located in this random audit are reported to them and the errors, plus or minus, are corrected.

Jones arbitrarily increased the total of one monthly expense account total by $100. He knew he could keep this if his expense accounts were not chosen for the audit that year. If caught in an audit, he knew it would simply be attributed to an error in addition on his part.

Jones's total increase of reported expenses over actual expenses this year was about 5%. He has no unusual expenses of a non-recurring nature.

QUESTIONS

1. Who ultimately pays the padded 5% in Jones's expense accounts?
2. Which of "Carson's Laws" is the company ignoring in its established expense reimbursement policy?
3. In future years, will Jones's expense account padding, under present reimbursement policies, probably
   > stay the same?
   > increase?
   > decrease?
4. What minimum action should the company take to prevent expense account padding?

Section II
THE APPLICATION OF SECURITY

Chapter 3

Cost Considerations in Security

In business one measure of the effectiveness of security is the degree of respect which employees hold for the employer's property. The effectiveness of management, in turn, can be measured by the amount of profit which is retained because security procedures promote a high degree of this respect.

Security is the state of being secure; in the context of this book, secure against theft by employees. *Total* security is not economically practical, even if man and science could guarantee it. Therefore, it is necessary to qualify this definition: *security in the business world is the state of being secure to the maximum extent that profits will sustain.*

Any security system will be less than total, but the ideal approach is to begin with a system planned to provide total security. Once such a plan is prepared, only slight modification is needed to make it economically practical and still effective.

A complete plan will cover marginal areas such as protection of property which would be difficult for a thief to dispose of. Examples include material whose bulk alone makes it impossible or too costly to transport. Other products may be so specialized in material, size or shape that their only market is the customer who ordered them.

In cutting back a total security system to an economical size, the first step should be to reduce or eliminate protection for materials yielding low financial return to the thief. Other than cash, stolen commodities lose at least half their value simply because they are stolen. There is generally no need to protect something which a thief cannot sell at a profit.

Different Problems, Different Security

Many of the examples in this book are drawn from employee dishonesty problems in the manufacturing business. Even this type of business often has many security problems not directly concerned with product theft or diversion. Different types of business, moreover, have altogether different types of security problems. Some of these, for example, will concern direct thefts of money. Because currency loses none of its value when stolen, it offers the greatest temptation to the thief.

A construction job experienced problems when an employee was hired and then discharged after one pay period. The employee quit working, but his name stayed on the payroll. The foreman approved his own payrolls and cashed employees' checks at the bank as a favor to them. He forged the signature of the discharged employee, cashed the checks and pocketed the proceeds.

In another case, a manufacturer of plumbing supplies operated a cash sales counter to sell its products to local plumbers. The sales were recorded on hand-written, unnumbered sales slips, with one copy going into the cash drawer with the money. The man operating this sales counter merely destroyed some sales ticket copies and put the money in his pocket.

One manufacturing company operated its own snack and soft drink stands, which were run by supervisors during work breaks. The company thought it was saving money by not installing vending machines. The supervisors were taking food without paying for it, and giving free food to their friends. In addition, some of the cash received from sales went into the supervisors' pockets.

There is no one security plan that covers all three of these examples. Security measures must be tailored to remove the temptations in a particular business.

Start With a Complete Security System

Even when the added cost of a fully effective security system seems too large, a complete system should be drawn up. The starting point should be a plan that covers all weak spots indicated in a security survey and tries to prevent all temptations to steal. Then the system can be scaled back by eliminating security in marginal areas where the protected material would have a low value to the thief.

The opposite approach, that of inching up to a full security system by protecting weak points as losses are discovered, is an expensive procedure that gives the thief all the advantages. Management never knows what the thief will try until he has already succeeded in doing so. If he is a smart thief, the company may never stumble onto his next plan.

On the other hand, a complete security system trimmed down to economical size will usually prevent an employee from trying a dishonest scheme. Where specific security procedures are effected to correct security weaknesses, and employees are kept constantly aware of the presence of the security department and its accomplishments, the employees are conditioned to stay honest.

Narrow Security Approach

The narrow approach to security tries to identify a thief without attempting to eliminate the temptation that induced the theft. It tries to catch one thief without trying to cut off the opportunities for theft which others may also take advantage of. A narrow approach adds to costs without any compensating preventive plan.

Example: A vending machine company had a number of routes providing food service in office buildings and industrial plants. Each route was charged for the total food put into its machines each day and received credit for the money turned in.

Unexpectedly, one route started showing a much smaller income than the amount of food should have produced. The route man was a long-time employee; he denied responsibility for the shortage, which continued after he was told about it. Supervisors could only verify that machines on this route did not produce enough money, and that no other routes were short.

The investigator called into the case suggested that a survey be made to determine what weaknesses were present in the business. Management refused this suggestion; they were sure the route man was guilty and they wanted only to prove his guilt so that a claim could be filed on their fidelity bond coverage.

As an emergency measure, the company insisted on checking the contents of the machines and their coin boxes just ahead of the route man on this particular route. Several days of this expensive effort showed that he was turning in the entire contents of the coin boxes.

Next, the company insisted on a surveillance of the route man to catch him making unscheduled trips back to the machines on his route. Several days of costly surveillance failed to discover any unscheduled trips to these machines.

Meanwhile, the investigator continued to suggest a survey be made to locate weak spots in the company's security. After the company had tried all the narrow approaches it could think of, with no results, they reluctantly agreed to a full security survey.

Since all trucks worked out of one building, where the general offices and stock room were located, this was the focal point for the survey. The survey began at the truck loading platform, to verify procedures for accounting for what was charged out of the stock room for each truck. There, in plain sight, was a large board with a hook for each route. Each route man hung up his keyring on the board at night and picked it up the next morning when he started out on his route.

For a predictable period each afternoon, and again each morning, the key board was full of keys available to anyone who walked past. A set of keys could be taken off the board at night, copies made, and the keys returned to the board early the next morning.

Two groups had access to the board at night. The contract janitorial service came in to clean after employees had left at the end of the day. Vending machine repairmen had keys to the building so they could obtain parts and tools when machines broke down at night. There were so many people with access to the key board, in fact, that it was surprising that only one route man was being robbed.

This problem was solved by division of responsibility so that no one person could obtain keys without at least one other person's permission. The keys were kept in a safe at night and the combination was changed and rotated among three men. Even collusion was limited to a period of one month unless all three of these men were involved. When these steps had been taken, the losses stopped.

The thief was never identified. Narrow security measures did not stop the thief. A security survey could have stopped losses earlier, at a lower cost.

In this example, route income had been compiled daily for accounting purposes, but comparison between routes was made only monthly. As a result of the security survey, one copy of the daily report went to the executive responsible for security. He made daily and cumulative reports on route income, and deviations from normal could be noted quickly. The reports, which had been intended originally for other purposes, now fulfilled a security function as well. As will be demonstrated in later chapters, many of the procedures in any good security system are based on reports which were already in existence for other purposes.

Negative Security Approach

Negative security attempts to punish someone, not necessarily the thief, for prior losses. All too often a security program is born from the shock of a large year-end inventory shortage. Usually the department or branch location where the loss occurred is known. Someone in management is discharged, demoted or transferred as punishment — not because he took anything, but because he allowed the loss to take place. All too often, this punishment is the entire security effort. Nothing is done to prevent the same thing happening again. Top management shows its ignorance of its responsibility to take positive action to prevent losses. Frustration at the loss of profit causes a negative, punitive reaction.

In some of these cases, management will take a further step

and try to identify the employee(s) who caused the previous year's inventory shortage. These attempts are costly and seldom succeed. This type of negative security does not correct the weakness in the system that invited the loss.

In some cases, investigation does identify the thieves and substantial recoveries are made. But in these cases there was a starting point — the method of theft or the thief's identity was known or strongly suspected in the beginning. Because they lack experience in such matters, management may not always recognize these starting points. A trained security staff has the necessary experience.

Even if the thief is caught, he rarely has sufficient assets to provide total recovery. Fidelity bonds are often the only source of recovered funds. Even when the method of theft and the thief's identity are known, it should always be the primary aim of security to prevent the same temptation from corrupting other employees. Punishment and recovery are important deterrents, but they cost more and deter less than prevention of temptation. The primary aim must always be to remove temptation.

Non-Theft Dishonesty

An inventory shortage does not necessarily mean a theft has taken place. This is another good reason for establishing accountability and changing the system before looking for the thief.

Example: A large lumber company had conducted an extensive investigation to find out who had stolen several million board feet of rough lumber that showed short in a year-end inventory. No thefts had been proven by a prior investigation, and the missing lumber did not show up in the lumber market. A private investigator was brought in to examine accounting records and other internal log and lumber flow records. The investigation indicated that more rough lumber was recorded as produced by the sawmill than the sawed logs could have contained.

Sawmills measure one end and the length of each log to compute the board feet of rough lumber the log will produce. This measurement is made on the log when it is received and again when it is taken out of the log stock pile. The log is measured in the same way by the sawmill foreman when it is sawed into rough lumber. No comparison was being made between these two measurements; the records went to different management levels. The log stock pile report (inventory of rough lumber in unsawed logs) went to the tree-cutting foreman to inform him how many trees had to be cut down to keep the stock pile even. The sawmill report went to a clerk in the accounting department who kept an inventory of rough lumber on hand.

In order to make his performance record more impressive, the sawmill foreman had been exaggerating his report of logs sawed. He was not stealing; he was just making himself look good. Yet he created a vexing problem for management, necessitating expensive investigations when the company could not account for several million board feet of lumber. Year-end statements for management and tax purposes would not balance because the inventory gap could not be explained. Since the cause of the discrepancy was unknown, no adjustment could be made in published statements.

After the investigation was completed, the company was able to make the necessary adjustment in rough lumber inventory. A minor change in the recording methods sent a copy of the stock pile report and the sawmill report to the inventory clerk. He prepared a running chart of the board feet of rough lumber in the log stock pile as shown by each report, and advised management if the two lines on this chart started to diverge. The added cost of making this comparison was negligible, and no new reports were required.

Although there was no loss of property in this case, any system that allows such variance in inventory reporting is also wide open to the thief. For example, the sawmill foreman could have *under*stated the rough lumber produced from each log, and then sold this difference for personal profit.

Like the earlier example of the vending machine company thefts, in the sawmill case the records that could provide the needed security measures were already being prepared for reasons other than security. A small change in distribution of existing records, or a modest increase in an employee's work load, can often increase security at little extra cost.

Security As An Expense

Security produces nothing that can be sold at a profit. Unfortunately, from management's point of view security shows up on a profit-and-loss statement as an expense only. A security system is therefore economical only when it offers management a return reasonably greater than the cost of the system.

If a company wants to build a good security system, however, it must be prepared to spend some money that may not provide much immediate return. Before any reductions in security are made simply to reduce immediate expense, management should consider the long-range effects of security measures on security costs.

A good security program essentially requires only two steps: (1) hire employees who are relatively honest; and (2) keep them honest. But this is a program of *prevention*. The increased honesty among employees that results from the security plan has a continuing and cumulative effect. It continues to produce more employee honesty at less cost year after year, long after employees forget why the security measures were instituted.

Unfortunately, moral considerations seem to come in second to immediate profits in most decisions on security. At the management level, moral bankruptcy is excused as the price of avoiding fiscal bankruptcy. Most employees, for their part, are motivated more by the size of the paycheck than by either morals or company profits. Management and employees each have a different standard, and neither begins with honesty.

A good security system, therefore, must show employees that dishonesty is likely to cut off their paychecks. At the same time, the security system can demonstrate to management that profits will not be impaired but may, in fact, be improved, because good security is cumulative. Honesty builds on itself and moral character is strengthened. Honesty, however achieved, breeds profits.

Dishonesty Limits Profits

Poor security measures permit dishonesty to flourish. While dishonesty is difficult to measure in dollars or in effect on profits, an employee discharged for dishonesty reflects a failure by management to use the employee's full potential. An employee must be ingenious to figure out a successful method of stealing. He has to know the system before he can plan a way to beat it. That extra ability could have been channeled into constructive use for the company. Good security measures should have waved a danger signal in that employee's face the first time he thought about a dishonest plan. He should have seen prison bars instead of dollar signs.

Example: The chattel mortgage loan section of a large bank experienced a $200,000 shortage. The bank official in charge of the section was capable and well informed about banking. He had been promoted because of his personality and abilities and was in line to be the next executive officer.

Other bank officers knew that the head of the chattel mortgage section was drinking heavily after work. They also knew he was betting a great deal on sporting events and losing money regularly in card games. Because of his favored position in the bank, however, these security risks went unreported.

In semi-annual internal cross-audits, the heads of various bank sections were assigned to audit other sections. These assignments were made at random as part of the security program. It had been so long since these audits had turned up any major dishonesty, however, that they had become routine exercises.

In past cross-audits, bank officials assigned to the chattel mortgage section, well aware of the favored position held by its head, were careful not to show him in an unfavorable light. Even though they found notes not properly signed, credit information missing, and car identification numbers left off of some purchase contracts, they did not report the irregularities.

A cross-audit of the chattel mortgage section was assigned to an officer who had been passed over in promotion in favor of the chattel mortgage officer. The assigned auditor was capable, thorough — and angry. Although the auditor did not suspect dishonesty, he felt that the chattel mortgage officer's personal life was not good for the bank's image. He decided to write up every minor error he found in the audit, including things other auditors had ignored.

He found that many of the chattel mortgage loans were made to people buying used cars from one particular dealer. Loans were made on many cars too old to be good loan risks, and the dealer seemed to have sold too many cars for the size of his lot.

The auditor segregated all the active loan ledger cards for this particular dealer. He noted that most of the cards had a special yellow tab on top that did not appear on other car dealers' cards. He made a list of these tabbed cards by note date and found that many loans were made on the same dates each month. The total of all payments made on the same date was almost the same as the total of new loans made the same date.

The auditor then contacted selected names from the loan records and found that the people had not bought the cars listed in the loans, had not signed notes and contracts, and had not received time payment books.

Since the loans were fictitious and caused false entries in bank records (a Federal criminal offense), the FBI was called in. The offending bank officer admitted to falsifying records. He had divided the proceeds with the used car dealer. The scheme had operated for at least two years without other employees of the section becoming suspicious. The loss to the bank was much larger than the amount of the fidelity bond on its employees. The loan section had to be completely reorganized. Some employees resigned and others were moved into other jobs at the bank. The chairman of the board lost face because the guilty man had been his protege.

The immediate monetary loss was the least of the bank's problems. It lost the guidance of the chairman of the board. A talented man, who had been capable of becoming the bank's executive officer, went wrong because he found it easy and profitable to steal.

The most important point illustrated by this case is that the dishonest acts touched everyone who worked in the bank. Morale was damaged; leadership was lost; depositors lost confidence. The officers who had conducted previous audits without reporting improper procedures faced a limited future. The overall loss was much greater than the cost of a security system that could have prevented the scheme.

Growth and Decentralization Increase Risks

A major loss through employee dishonesty often can be traced to some change in management structure. Often this change is simply growth. A small, personally operated business where the owner knows his employees grows into a larger business where the number of employees makes a personal relationship impossible. Employees will not be so quick to steal from an owner who is a personal friend; they often see nothing wrong with stealing from an impersonal corporation.

Growth also decentralizes functions and authority. Security under one roof is maintained without much effort simply because the boss sees more — and is seen more. Branch locations and separated operations result in decentralized purchasing, hiring, shipping and other functions previously under personal observation. The boss is less in view; control is watered down. Increased security should always accompany any expansion.

Example: A major oil and gas producer hired a team of investigators after discovering serious kickback problems. This case typifies most of the security problems inherent in decentralized operations.

Roads could not be built in the marshland coastal areas where oil wells were being drilled. Central supply and service areas were miles away from the drilling rig; the crew lived on barges at the drilling sites. Each drilling operation was almost entirely free of centralized supervision.

The drilling superintendent on each rig bought all his own supplies, including food and drilling mud. It was common practice for the local store that supplied food for the crew kitchen to supply free groceries to the drilling superintendent's home. The store paid kickback in kind.

Drilling mud was bought in dry form in sacks and made into mud at the rig. The mud was forced down the drill pipe to serve as lubricant for the drill bit and to bring debris from the bit to the surface. Often the drill bit would hit a thick layer of salt. The water in the mud would dissolve the salt and the mud would spread out underground so that pressure could not be maintained. The problem was solved by saturating the mud with salt so that it could not absorb any underground salt. This process required tremendous quantities of salt. If the supplier shorted each load by ten bags of salt, the shortage would not be noted when the invoice was paid, as long as the invoice was approved by the superintendent. The drilling company paid for undelivered salt; the supplier and the superintendent divided the extra money.

Since there were no roads in the area, final delivery to the rig was made by a contract boat service which the superintendent arranged locally. Some superintendents went into partnership in boat rental companies and approved payment for boat time not used.

Suppliers were paid for materials and services they did not furnish. These excess payments were run through suppliers' records along with legitimate payments. The suppliers paid about half to the drilling superintendent in person and retained the rest for their participation in the scheme.

These kickbacks by the supplier were sometimes paid in cash but more often were in the form of supplies or appliances. Many superintendents drove cars owned by suppliers. In one case, the superintendent could not show payment for the house he had built nor for any of its furnishings.

Many of the headquarters officials had once been drilling superintendents who themselves accepted kickbacks. Newly assigned superintendents merely took over previously established kickback arrangements. Superintendents promoted to higher jobs made no move to stop the practice.

Although kickback payments such as these usually start in great secrecy, as they become habitual they increase in size and greed supersedes secrecy. Others down the line in supervision see their boss getting rich and they start their own, smaller sideline dishonesties. The boss cannot do much about it without the risk of having his own dishonesties exposed. The disease sets in, costs rise, profits decline, and the honesty of many employees is eroded.

Separated operations are usually set up with no plan for extending security. The central office cannot exercise control in the branches, and the greater freedom granted those in charge of the separated operation introduces greater temptation. When, in the interest of "economy," security fails to keep pace with company growth and decentralization, the proliferation of employee dishonesty creates a far greater drain on profits than the cost of preventive security measures.

Conclusions

1. A company's degree of security is measured by the degree of respect employees hold for company property.

2. The degree of employee honesty desired determines the kind and amount of security a company will need.

3. The cost of security measures must be related to the profits they produce or the losses they prevent.

CASE HISTORY #2

The Arctura Corporation has a manufacturing branch in a city where material components are available from local sources. This is not a large operation; everything is contained under one roof. There is no general security plan. A large general components shortage was disclosed by a year-end inventory.

Arctura hired a local private investigator to determine which employees had been stealing the components. This investigation, which lasted several weeks, was unproductive.

The investigation then turned to trying to locate the places in the plant where the material disappeared. This also was not productive because flow records for some parts were automatically destroyed after six months. The branch manager was brought back to headquarters and demoted because of the shortage.

QUESTIONS

1. Why is an attempt to catch a past thief a narrow approach to security?
2. What should Arctura have done first when the shortages were discovered at year-end?
3. In what two ways did Arctura's narrow approach fail?
4. What might be the expected effects on the branch plant of demoting the branch manager?

Chapter 4

Security Personnel and Functions

A security system must be continually reviewed and updated if it is to continue to discourage employee dishonesty. Otherwise today's positive action becomes tomorrow's routine and next week's open temptation. The observance of security regulations should be verified constantly; in addition, the regulations themselves should be reviewed periodically to determine their continued usefulness. The thief should not be the first to discover a weakness in security. Maintaining employee honesty requires that security change and grow with business change and growth.

Security's Status in the Company

Security should be isolated from influence by any one of the other parallel departments in a company. The desired level of security will seldom be maintained if the security function is assigned as a secondary job to an executive with more pressing responsibilities. If business size permits, the security chief should be independent of all other functions. He should report directly to the chief executive as do other department heads. If he must have other duties, these should concern equipment, local deliveries, plant housekeeping or something else not vital to overall security. These other duties should not require him to police himself.

The person responsible for security should be part of the executive team. He should be aware of changes that are planned in the business so that he can adjust security measures accordingly. No gaps should be left in security because of changing procedures. It is always cheaper to plan ahead than to try to catch up. Prevention of dishonesty is always cheaper than catching some of the thieves after the fact.

The security chief should be given the authority to enforce security measures. Management should decide how important security is to the company and then provide the authority to enforce it at that level.

STAFFING THE DEPARTMENT

The Security Chief

The chief of security must be a person capable of operating on the executive level. He must have the ability to translate a security survey into a security program. He must be sufficiently interested in his work to instill enthusiasm in the people who work for him.

As an executive, he should not be uniformed. The uniform expresses a policing power which is not appropriate for the chief, who operates at the level where reason and executive authority provide his power.

It is always cheaper in the long run to promote from within than to hire from without. For the position of security chief, however, as in technical fields, experience and prior training are primary requirements. The prospective executive must have security or police experience, along with some administrative experience. He must be able to function at a desk. Ability to work with business records and reports is vital to his role.

If a present employee is to be promoted to this job, the promotion should be made as a reward for ability — not because the employee is not performing adequately in his present position but has too much seniority to be discharged. The position of security chief is likewise not the place for an untrained, semi-retired individual who has suffered physical disability on the job. The chief of security must have the knowledge and ability to maintain employee honesty.

A good security chief should pick and train those who work under him. He should not be forced to accept anyone who cannot perform as the program requires. Too many security men are paid minimum wages because they are not worth more. The chief should have some authority over wage scales for his employees. The guard's uniform alone is not sufficient to promote honesty among employees. The person in that uniform must inspire enough respect so that employees will consider him a bar to dishonesty.

Drawbacks of Unqualified Security Staff

In one company in which a security survey was made, all uniformed guards were former production employees who had been injured on the job or were too inept to perform on the production line. Most had relatives working in the plant or office. They were paid the minimum wage plus small longevity increases. Those with longer service were made supervisors. The chief was the man with the most seniority.

Two things were very wrong here. Uniformed guards had the greatest opportunity for dishonesty because of the nature of their duties. Because of their low job status, pay scale and ability, they provided no barrier to dishonesty by other employees. The guards, in fact, were found to be more dishonest than most other employees.

Other situations illustrate the potential cost of an unqualified security force:

• The New York Port Authority once reported they caught their guards stealing more often than those same guards caught others stealing.

• In New Orleans, a dock watchman was the reported head of an interstate theft ring. A search of his home revealed a veritable department store of stolen goods.
• A grocery store chain caught a guard acting as a wholesale supplier of liquor to small bars. He merely loaded case lots, on order, into the trunk of his car while on weekend duty.

A guard should have the education and ability to command a pay scale at least equal to that of those employees whose honesty he supervises. His job requires the ability to make proper decisions in emergencies or when there is no one else available to make those decisions. Other employees must respect guards for their ability to protect against proposed dishonesties. A guard's ability should be at least as strong a deterrent factor as his uniform.

Security Inspectors

Although few security departments in the past have included the position of security inspector, this function can be a valuable part of an overall security program. An *inspector* is one who looks at things carefully. Everyone is familiar with production line inspectors. The security department needs inspectors who are trained to know and capable of inspecting business procedures and business forms.

The chapters in Section III dealing with accountability in purchasing, receiving, sales and shipping describe a system best operated by such inspectors. Independent verification and comparison of various records are needed to attain accountability. Security inspectors are responsible for the success of this system. They are independent of control by other departments. Their job is to maintain the honesty of employees in those departments by this system of inspection.

Because the inspectors need to be able to follow the normal flow paths of those records, they will usually be drawn from accounting or other office staffs. Their qualifications should include a desire to be part of the security effort. Knowledge of the business they will inspect is of primary importance. Curiosity and imagination are other important attributes for this position. The inspectors need not be uniformed. They deal more with records than with people.

Other Staffing Policies

The security chief should be a salaried executive like the heads of other departments. The inspection personnel and those under the chief who have authority over lower level guards should also be salaried. This applies to all uniformed personnel not assigned to or relieving on duty posts. Their salaried position adds to their status of command over those they must keep honest and indicates recognition of their increased responsibilities.

Guards and relieving supervisors who man posts are subject to longer and irregular hours. They should be paid on an hourly basis so they can be compensated for extra or unusual hours. Since manning a guard post is usually not physically strenuous, there is no drop in efficiency with reasonable overtime work. It is often better to pay overtime to regular employees than to hire and train extra guards who will work less than a full schedule.

The security staff should make most applicant investigations for the personnel department. These can be made either by inspectors or guard supervisors. Applicants for jobs in the security department should be investigated by someone already in a higher position than that of the applicant.

Planned Expansion

The security department must expand with a growing business. Production expansion always presents new security problems. A new building changes the flow of personnel and materials. Accountability checkpoints may change. Trash collection and pickup may need to be changed because of increased security vulnerabilities.

Special security risks are involved in branch office expansion. A system may work well in a centralized plant, yet fail in branch locations. Local conditions may threaten a branch although the same conditions would be no risk to a larger plant. A small branch may not be able to afford protection by uniformed guards when it is closed. Alarms may be installed for protection during unmanned closed hours. Surrounding conditions may cause increased fire hazards.

Security expansion must be planned as other parts of the business expand. Security should be included in the planning phases so that it can perform its function when the expansion takes place.

SECURITY FUNCTIONS IN ACCOUNTABILITY

Accountability Verification

Section III of this book deals with the use of normal business forms to prevent employee dishonesty. Accountability requires that forms and reports from two or more separate functions prove that what is purchased and paid for is received; that it is accounted for in production; and that what is produced is sold and paid for. The security department provides the verification of these accountability factors. This is the primary function of the inspection personnel.

The security inspectors verify that all pre-numbered forms are accounted for. They destroy the pre-numbered forms when they have served their purpose. They verify the transition from the end of old numbered forms to the start of a new numbered series. They check entries in the sales order register book against the forms recorded there, and they check the forms on individual orders to be sure the information on all forms agrees.

All these functions are detailed under chapter headings in Section III. These chapters generally follow the departmental set-up of a manufacturing business from requisitions for material to payment for sales. Security inspectors turn static records into proof of accountability.

Check Lists

Accountability requires verification of certain procedures. What is ordered must be received in the same quantity, quality, and at the same price as it was ordered. What is put into production must appear in the finished product or be consumed in production. Sales must equal production minus inventory, and must be paid for. Multiple independent verification procedures toward these ends are set out in Section III.

A plan for verification does not in itself provide accountability. *Independent verification of the execution of the plan* provides accountability. Security check lists can provide the required independent verification.

These check lists will be printed forms. Each separate form will verify one or more counts of materials, one or more applicant statements, or one or more job performance functions. For example, check lists can verify:

- That a supplier's invoice shows the same quantity, quality and price shown on the purchase order.
- That the receiving tally, requisition and purchase order quantities agree.
- That the stockroom received what the requisition called for.
- That the dates, places and types of former employment listed by an applicant on his employment application are accurate.
- That fire protection equipment is in working order.
- That gate guards are performing properly all the duties set out in their post manual.
- That the complete numerical sequence of each pre-numbered form is accounted for.

The printed forms for check lists will show the type and place of each verification, the records to be used and the commodity or statement to be verified. Space will then be provided to show date of verification, quantity or statement verified, any deviations and action required by the deviations. Each form will be signed by the inspector who fills it out.

REQUISITION CHECK LIST

Requisition No. _____   Requisition Date _____
Issuing Department _____
Purchase Order No. _____   P. O. Date _____
Supplier _____
Receiving Tally No. _____   Tally Date _____
Supplier Invoice No. _____Date Paid _____Check No. _____

Inspection Detail:

The completed purchase order package shows that requisition,
purchase order, receiving tally and supplier's invoice agree as to
quantity and quality; that the purchase order, supplier's invoice
and payment check agree in dollar value, and that material
received in the stock room matches the original requisition.

Date of Inspection _____   Inspector _____
If there are any deviations in any of the above items note them here with your
recommendations for remedial action.

Date of Inspection _____   Inspector _____

Figure 1. Sample Check List Form

Figure 1 is a typical example of a check list form.

Except for employment application verification (covered fully in Section III, Chapter 8), these check lists will not provide 100% verification of all named functions. Check lists for materials and job performance will provide for spot checks at irregular times. Frequency will be determined by the number and importance of variations shown by prior check lists.

Check lists should be rotated so that one inspector does not check the same function time after time. The timing and assignment of check list inspections should not become routine. Neither employees nor inspectors should be able to gauge when checks will be made or who will make them.

Check lists should be retained long enough to permit their use if shortages show up at a later stage. Checking these lists back along a production line will help pinpoint the area where the shortage occurred. This may also show where some security inspector failed to do his job properly.

Auditing of Check Lists

No department should police itself; this includes the security department. The check lists should be audited by someone at the executive level outside of security. These audits should compare check lists at succeeding stations in purchasing, production and sales to ensure that no shortages go unreported, that check list entries are complete, and that checking does not become routine in date or execution.

This outside policing of security should concentrate on security's performance and not on its policies. Security policy should be set at the executive level where other business policy is set.

Auditing of the security check lists should require review of all deviations noted and follow-up on corrective measures taken. The auditing answers two separate questions:

1. Is the security department providing security?
2. Do any deviations noted by security require corrective action by management?

The executive level is somewhat isolated from day-to-day activity at lower levels. Security inspections can provide information for executives which they cannot obtain for themselves. Production deviations on check lists will indicate a dishonesty or a weakness. Weaknesses and poor supervision can be noted and corrected; dishonesty can be punished.

Security Reports

The previous discussion of check lists and their audits was concerned with verifying that the security department is checking and testing activity of other departments. But security's performance must also be monitored, and for this reason security reports should be required on the department's own functions.

The security department will be responsible to some higher executive and will provide that executive with regular reports of its activities. One of these reports will record what check lists have been prepared, what deviations were found, what corrective actions were taken, and what future action is recommended.

Another report will deal with any security deficiencies caused by changing production methods, changing employee totals, use of different shipping methods, new raw materials, and anything else that requires different security methods. This report should be made regularly at stated intervals so that management will be aware of how changes they make affect security. This report should be made even when it states only that no security changes are necessary.

Another regular report should be prepared on the status of fire security. Management will look on a new raw material only from the standpoint of its greater profit-making potential. Security will recognize its greater fire hazards.

Operations may require other reports as the security department faces new or different security problems. Top level management should know what the security department does and how it does it.

SPECIAL INVESTIGATIONS

Undercover Employees

Any large employer will sometimes need information from within his plant that his own security staff cannot provide. There are legal and moral limitations on the type of information which can be obtained from undercover sources. Following is one example of the legitimate use of undercover operatives.

The new manager of a large wood products manufacturer found certain work groups, such as the shipping department, were highly over-staffed. To discover why, he arranged for an undercover source of information within the shipping department. He soon learned that the foreman of the department was the local leader of the Ku Klux Klan. The foreman hired only Klan members and hired two for every job, so that all made an easy living.

An undercover employee works at a regular job and receives his paycheck in the same manner and amount as other employees in similar positions. He must perform this regular job so that his fellow employees do not suspect his undercover role. He is paid extra for his undercover activity. There should be one person only who supervises his activity. He reports to that person and receives his extra pay from that person. He must be protected completely from detection.

There are many theft situations where undercover investigation is the only way to identify the employee thief. This is particularly true where a conspiracy exists involving several employees.

The security department should supervise undercover activity to prevent its use for unlawful or unethical purposes, to terminate it when its purpose is served, and to prevent any company official from using it for personal reasons. Undercover work has a limited function and should never exceed that function. The security department should report each undercover investigation to a top executive who must authorize the extra payment before it is made.

Undercover employees need special training in avoiding detection, procedures for reporting and limitations of authority before they can safely produce the desired information. They need to know how thieves operate. This type of experience is seldom found among regular employees. A regular employee is also likely to have friends and relatives among the other employees. He will be reluctant to inform about them. He might furnish management with enough information to seemingly justify his payment for undercover work, while still protecting an organized theft ring.

The best sources of undercover employees are those private investigative organizations that specialize in undercover investigation or provide it in conjunction with other services. There are several national firms and other local groups throughout the U.S. The major advantages of these sources are the training and supervision they supply their employees. They also provide greater isolation for the undercover employee and thereby protect him from discovery.

In order for the undercover operative to be hired in the first place, it is usually necessary for one supervisor to know his identity. This supervisor should have no contact with him thereafter except as a regular employee. The supervisor may be curious about what the undercover employee is looking for, but the reasons for the investigation should not be divulged to him. The supervisor will then have one less reason for contacting the undercover employee about his undercover work. If such contact is made, the undercover employee should report it, and the supervisor should be cautioned about making such contacts.

Private Investigations

Local, routine applicant investigations can often be done most cheaply and quickly by the company's own security staff. Outside investigations of employee theft are better made by private investigators. They will have greater experience and more outside contacts than the company's own staff. Their activity can be more anonymous since no one need know the reasons for their questions. The company's interest need not be exposed.

Private investigators will be equipped for surveillance work. They can obtain information from distant sources without the time and expense of sending a man for it. Their investigations will be impartial. They can be hired as needed. Using outside investigators avoids the problem of taking staff members off their regular assigned work for intermittent tasks.

Most cities will have a choice of private investigation agencies available, many of which employ investigators with police or FBI experience. In small communities where experienced investigators are not available, personnel can be sought from a nearby city.

Rates for private investigation vary. The cheapest are usually cheap because of their lack of ability. The company should be willing to pay for experience and ability. A definite agreement should be made about hourly rates and expense, and a maximum total price should be set. Quotes may be obtained from several agencies to determine which will get the job done adequately at a reasonable price.

Investigative reports should not contain much detail about the methods by which the information was obtained. The source and the information itself are important. Other details should be given only if they help to evaluate the information obtained. Payment should never be based on the length of the report.

It is illegal to use private investigators to obtain information about union activities. Telephone taps are also illegal. In some states, microphone installations can be used on company property to gather information about illegal activities. If a company is considering microphone use, it should have an attorney research the situation. Generally, information obtained in this manner cannot be used in court or in punitive actions against employees where such action becomes public. Local police should be called upon to develop the evidence for court or other punitive action.

OTHER SECURITY RESPONSIBILITIES

The security staffing and special functions briefly discussed in this chapter are by no means the entire picture of security operations. A major area of protection responsibility is physical security, which is directed toward the prevention of external attack as well as internal losses.

It is not within the scope of this book to attempt a detailed study of physical security, about which volumes have been written. However, a general review of physical security, with special attention to those areas which affect employee honesty and accountability, is important enough to deserve separate discussion in the chapter that follows.

CASE HISTORY #3

Arctura's security system grew as Arctura grew but was limited to physical security. The first gate guard hired was a retired policeman with no prior specialized training or experience in plant security. Other uniformed guards were added as the plant grew. They were all former employees from the plant or relatives of other guards. The first guard was designated boss of the other guards because of his seniority. He had no training except that gained on the job. He had no training program for the other guards.

Arctura Corporation started with a one-man executive staff — the owner. He knew everyone who worked for him in the early years of operation. As the corporation grew he continued this patriarchal interest in the employees but soon lost his personal contacts with them. Branch operations were completely separated from this personal contact.

Arctura obviously needed to update its security system. The problems at the branch plant described in Case History #2 finally caused Arctura to plan such an update.

QUESTIONS

1. What background should be required for a new chief of security?
2. Should the security chief be a salaried or an hourly wage employee? Why?
3. Should post guards be paid a salary or a wage? At what level of pay? Why?
4. At what point should security planning begin for a new branch plant?

Chapter 5

Mechanics of Physical Security

Physical security refers to protection obtained by visible, material means. It originated from the concept of a guarded wall to prevent attack from outside. Many businesses still think of physical security in terms of barriers aimed outward, fencing out those who would enter without permission. Some of these barriers are easily adapted to work both ways; directed inward, they help deter employee dishonesty.

These barriers are usually rigid in their application; consequently, little judgment is required to implement them. Security is needed at a particular point, and a person or a device provides it. Violations are noted quickly, and pre-determined corrective action is taken.

Uniformed guards are an integral part of this system. They observe violations, evaluate their severity and determine the degree of response required. Because guards are not engaged in production duties, however, many other functions have devolved on them. Their policing authority, visibly exemplified in their uniforms and equipment, also aids in control of people in the plant area.

Physical Security Evolution

Man's earliest attempts at living peacefully with his fellow man probably arose from the need to protect his immediate family group and his few hunting tools and weapons from intruders. Survival made the procurement of food man's most important and ever-present need. Family groups joined together for mutual protection; certain men became guards while others hunted food. The hunters produced something of value, while the guards produced nothing. Theirs was a secondary function; they merely protected what was produced by others.

With the development of agriculture, man lived where his crops grew. His community increased in size and his possessions grew in number and importance. He built walled areas into which he could retreat when attacked. The walls were manned to provide constant protection for the homes and possessions of the farmers and artisans. The guards were important because their mere presence discouraged attack, but since they did not produce anything of substance, their position remained below that of those who did produce food or goods.

Today's uniformed security guard is the direct descendant of man's early efforts to protect his family and possessions. He still produces nothing tangible, and his position is below that of the producer. He is paid less; his function is thought to be less important. Too often today he is a partially disabled production employee, or one who failed to become proficient in running a production machine, or someone's relative who needs a job but lacks skills. Physical security as a trade suffers from its origin as a subordinate function, a non-producer in a society that gives the big prizes to producers. It suffers from being considered a necessary evil.

Government Contract Influence

As World War II approached, the federal government became directly involved in production of war materiel. The need to protect war production from enemy action led to development of an entirely new concept of security and the uniformed guard. The ever-present enemy threat to national security upgraded the importance of the uniformed guard where government contracts were involved. The guard's cost was no longer considered only a reduction in profits; it became another factor in the price paid by the government for necessary war supplies. In fact, in cost-plus-percentage contracts, a higher-paid guard actually helped profits.

The government established higher standards of competence for security guards by establishing higher standards of security. Security became so important that cost became a secondary factor. The protection of war materiel became as important as its production. The men who provided this protection became as important as the men who produced the equipment. These wartime security procedures have continued in some respects in requirements on all later government contracts, whether defense-connected or not.

The experience with competent security guards on government contracts taught some companies to respect the usefulness of guards in non-government production. Other companies maintain competent uniformed guards because they hope to obtain government contracts in the future. It is cheaper to be prepared than to have to upgrade the guard force after a government contract is awarded.

These factors have caused some general improvement in the status of uniformed guards, but for the most part they are still the non-producers who are considered to be entitled only to a minimum wage. Economically, the high wartime standards for guards can be maintained only where the cost can be passed on to the customer.

Those who have improved their security because of government contracts know that such security reduces loss. These reduced losses, and the improvement in employee honesty that follows, have been demonstrated. Improvement in the general status of uniformed guards has resulted from the recognition that better security generally means better profits.

This has been a slow improvement in which the profit factor has been more important than the moral factor of increased employee honesty. But there are now fewer disabled employees being retired to the guard force. Training courses for guards are being instituted. Security directors are becoming part of the management team. Schools and colleges provide both in-class and on-the-job training for guard supervisors.

Uniformed Guard Duties

The guard's duties will vary according to what has to be protected and the physical plant layout. Much has been written on this single subject. There are professional associations that deal only with these problems and their practical solutions. In the entire field of industrial and commercial security, the use of barriers and uniformed guards in physical security has received more attention than all other security problems combined. Because of the wide experience already recorded in this area, the details will not be repeated here. There are, however, certain basic functions that deserve emphasis.

No static physical barrier performs its protective function unless it is supervised by a person. This may be as simple as a guard checking a door at night to be sure it is locked, or it can be as sophisticated as manning a closed circuit television monitoring station to watch an entire perimeter fence. The eyes and ears of the person make sure that no barrier has been breached; that gates are used only for authorized purposes; and that employees follow security and safety regulations. In its ultimate sophisticated form, a computer system may be used to lock and unlock doors, detect fires, control lights and observe employee activity. Such a system can be monitored from one console. There must still be a man to watch the monitor. Even the most secure and sophisticated systems, such as those used in maximum security prisons, depend on men to note and record activity.

In its simplest form, security is a uniformed guard patrolling a plant at night when no one else is there. So much depends on personnel in security systems that such security should rest on competent people who are ably supervised. This competence may vary according to what must be guarded and whom it must be guarded against.

For example, a uniformed guard in a retail store accomplishes a large part of his guard function simply by being in uniform where he can be seen. The authority of his uniformed presence alerts would-be thieves that management is aware of their threat. A lower grade of competence is required for this effort than is required to guard an armored car containing thousands of dollars in cash.

Separating Office from Plant

Perimeter protection is primary to all physical security for two reasons. It must protect against intrusion by unauthorized persons, and it must provide control of the movement of employees within the area. The first reason is well recognized and is a basic part of all physical security systems. The control of employees and people authorized to be within the perimeter is not as widely understood.

There must be close coordination between office and plant, but their physical operations should be separated for security reasons. Accountability cannot be obtained completely by use of partitions and locked doors. Office workers should not pass through the plant area on their way to restrooms or vending machines. The number of doors between office and plant should be kept to the minimum required for communication and supervision. The doors should be supervised to prevent unauthorized use. Those required to use the doors should be located near them so they will not have to wander around outside their work area. The number of people permitted to travel between the office and plant should be kept to a minimum. They should be identified by specially colored badges so it is necessary only to look at the color to see if a strange badge is in an unauthorized location.

Each trip between these locations should have a legitimate purpose and should be limited to that purpose. Visiting between employees only reduces the employees' production and is a threat to security. Any successful evasion of accountability between office and plant requires collusion between two people. Collusion should not be encouraged by allowing office and plant personnel to mingle on the job for non-productive or personal reasons.

Automobile Parking Areas

Good security requires that production employees park their personal cars outside the fenced security area. There is less of a security need for office employees to park away from their office area, but they should not park where they must walk through the plant to get to the office. In large plants it may be necessary to have more than one parking area for production employees. These parking lots should be distributed so that production employees have only a short walk to the time clock or guard gate admitting them to their work area.

There should always be a cleared area between the plant perimeter fence and the employee parking lots. Plant employees should not be permitted to return to their cars during working hours except through guard-attended gates. Fire doors and other emergency exits should be equipped with simple emergency exit bell alarms to alert security if they are used for unauthorized purposes. The same system can be used for regular entrance and exit doors so that a guard can activate the alarm bell if he must leave his post in an emergency. If an employee has a legitimate reason for leaving his plant area, he can call a guard to turn off the alarm. This will prevent plant employees from carrying small tools or other company property out to their automobiles.

Cars delivering employees to work or picking them up after work should never be permitted into the fenced plant area. Besides the security risk involved, there is also an insurance risk every time such a car drives into the plant area. Non-employee injuries are not covered by workmen's compensation insurance.

Time Clock Stations

Time clocks in themselves are not security devices. The gates through which employees pass on their way to or from work are security devices. They should be single-file gates and should be attended by uniformed guards whenever they are unlocked.

Good security requires uniformed guards in attendance at all time clock gates to deter dishonest practices. Employees who arrive late may have another employee punch in for them at the proper time. In some isolated work areas an employee can record arrival and departure on two or more time cards so that other employees will be paid for time not worked.

Badges and Passes

Many companies now photograph all new employees. The photos may be combined with other identifying data on the employee's badge. Cameras made for this purpose can combine a color photo with the identifying data in one exposure. Large departmentalized plants can color-code these badges so that all employees who use the same entrance gate and stay in the same work area have the same color badge. Another color can designate a danger area where hard hats must be worn or where no smoking is permitted. A strange badge can thus be spotted easily, and at a distance, by security personnel. Employees cannot trade badges because their photographs are included. Issuing badges of the same color to all employees entering a particular gate enables the security guard to make a fast check during rush periods.

Because some companies have eliminated time clocks, the importance to security of employee photographs and color-coded badges has increased. The color code can keep office personnel out of plant areas. Outside truck drivers making delivery or pickup will be spotted if they wander around the plant without a badge.

Lunch Box Searches

Tools, welding rods, copper wire and other small company property fit easily into a lunch box. These items are usually stolen for personal use. The potential loss is great because of the number of employees involved. To be really effective, lunch box inspections should be made after employees have lined up at an exit gate.

In two known instances where this was done, about half of the first 15 or 20 employees whose lunch boxes were searched were found to be guilty of small thefts. Nothing was found in lunch boxes further back in the line, but the ground was littered with similar items removed from lunch boxes by employees before reaching the search area.

This type of inspection need not be repeated often, nor need it be done to everyone in line. A search of about 10 to 15 lunch boxes at random in the line about once a week is usually sufficient warning to those tempted to steal in this manner. About once a month, every lunch box in the line should be checked. The fact that no one knows when or where a search will be made becomes part of accountability. Most employees will be influenced to resist the temptation to steal. If any employee is caught stealing during one of the searches, he should be assessed some pre-arranged penalty. Proper warning of the penalty for such thefts will make it possible to eliminate dishonest employees from the payroll.

This type of inspection should extend to all packages carried out by employees. In cold weather the search should include opening all heavy coats and jackets for eye inspection.

It is sometimes claimed that package searches violate a person's right to privacy. However, no employee has a right to steal his employer's property. The employment agreement should contain a statement, signed by the applicant, that he recognizes the employer's right to protect his property, and that, if hired, the applicant will voluntarily submit to such searches. These searches are justified if even one piece of stolen property is found. If two successive searches turn up no stolen property, the searches can be discontinued for some time. However, they should not be abandoned permanently.

Package searches should be made by the uniformed guards normally stationed at employee gates as part of their policing activity. Employees will be more likely to accept the search as a regular part of the guards' security function. The security department should also take part in any punitive action resulting from the searches. Security must have enforcement status before its lesser functions are respected.

Gate Guards

Besides the personnel entrances, gates are required for vehicles and visitors. These gates will be open only during normal business hours. No visitors should be admitted to the plant area without supervision, and no vehicles should enter without being authorized and logged in. This means that all open gates must be manned by uniformed guards. The greatest security control comes from the least number of gates; the greatest security economy comes from manning the least number of posts.

Empty trucks coming in to pick up shipments must enter and leave through one or more specified gates. Each truck should leave by the same gate through which it entered. (Specific reasons for this regulation are detailed in Chapter 15.) Trucks making deliveries of manufacturing materials and supplies should also enter and leave by the same specified gate for similar security reasons.

Trucks servicing vending machines or mechanical equipment should also use a specified gate. They should be inspected closely as they leave to be sure they contain no plant property. Company-owned trucks should also use specified gates and should never leave the plant without written authority. One copy of this authorization should be retained by the guard for later matching by the security department with a copy supplied by the supervisor issuing the authority. Verification from two unrelated sources provides accountability.

In some plants, bulk raw materials arrive regularly by truck or rail. These deliveries become so routine that supervision becomes lax. Security should recognize this danger and rotate security personnel so that no guard stays on the same gate long enough to let his duties become routine. This also prevents a guard from becoming too friendly with drivers who come and go regularly by one gate.

Gates serving railroad sidings should be locked when not in use. There should always be a uniformed guard on duty when rail gates are unlocked. Loaded railroad cars should not be left in the plant area for pickup by railroad employees after hours. Loaded cars should be left where railroad employees will not have access to the plant when picking up the cars. A guard should always supervise the removal of these cars and lock the rail gate as soon as they are removed.

Service Employee Control

Although service trucks and their drivers are so much a part of the normal routine that they are often not recognized as a security problem, they pose a threat to company property if they are permitted free access to the plant. Just as materials and completed products are protected from theft by dishonest employees and by outsiders, they also need to be protected from service employees.

Vending machines are becoming increasingly common in plant areas, often taking the place of other types of food service. Having vending machines in various locations accessible to work areas reduces employee time spent in reaching them and improves morale.

All vending machines require daily servicing. Because of the bulk of the items dispensed, service trucks must go to the machine locations. This means that service trucks have almost unlimited access to plant areas.

Vending machines should be located so that they are not adjacent to valuable property. The vending machine areas themselves can be fenced off from the surrounding plant so people patronizing or servicing them do not have a chance to wander into plant areas. All service trucks should enter and leave by one gate. The guard at this gate should look into the interior of each departing truck to be sure it contains no plant property.

Perimeter Security

Mechanical and electronic devices are being used increasingly for perimeter protection. Pressure sensors, light beams, electronic detectors, closed circuit television and other sophisticated equipment are replacing the foot patrol. These devices are harder for the criminal to avoid because they are always on station, ready to report any intrusion. Economic considerations, however, do not always favor the installation of elaborate security devices. They can be more expensive than one guard's salary and they still require personal supervision. Someone must be there to answer an alarm or to watch a console. Many well-locked and lighted buildings may need no more protection than that provided by regular police or private patrols. The value of the property that could be stolen, and the disruption of production that their loss would cause, are decisive factors.

Exterior lighting is the single most common method used in providing perimeter security. Low installation and operating costs bring this protection within the limits of most security budgets. The main problem is that most lights illuminate the perimeter and not the buildings to be protected. A passing patrolman cannot see anyone breaking into the plant; the lights may blind him so he cannot see the plant at all. Someone lurking in the shadows next to the building cannot be observed. The best systems use diffused general lighting aimed toward the buildings, with high intensity lights at the gates and doors.

Key Control

Unless a business operates around the clock every day of the year, at times it probably depends on locks alone as a form of security. Lights and patrol activity are used to guard the plant at night, in addition to locks, but during closed daylight hours there is often no backup for the locks.

Example: A store suffering regular unexplained losses had failed to pick up the door key from a discharged management employee. Every Sunday he merely opened up the store and took what he needed.

Laxity with keys can cause loss to any type of business. How many keys are there to the door or gate? Who has them? Are keys picked up from terminated employees? When were the locks last changed? Often no real record is kept and no one knows who has keys to the present locks. Good security requires that keys be under tight control.

Master Key Systems

Master key systems available today offer great flexibility. Properly used, they provide a high degree of security. Systems will vary according to security needs and the complexity of the areas to be locked.

Locks are usually associated with the older metal key systems, but locking systems are available today in which there are no keys. Locks may be activated by pushbuttons which must be pressed in proper sequence, or by insertion of an electronically encoded plastic card. These systems provide greater flexibility than conventional metal key systems because of the ease of changing codes. In another flexible type of locking system, a guard at a console views a closed circuit television monitor and unlocks doors or gates by remote control for authorized people. The very flexibility of this system easily leads to misuse. It should be used only in minimum security areas or for non-working hours, such as weekends.

Following is a list of sample recommendations about lock and key security made after a survey of a complex plant containing many manufacturing and administrative buildings.

1. In the administrative buildings, all doors leading to the parking lot or to the streets should be equipped with deadbolt locks requiring them to be locked with a key.

2. All doors leading from these administrative buildings to the plant area should be equipped with bolts on the inside so that the doors can be bolted by the security department after the buildings are closed at the end of the day. This will prevent unauthorized access from the plant into these buildings.

3. Soon after these administrative buildings are closed at the end of the working day, a roundsman should test all front doors to make sure they are locked. He should fasten the bolts on all doors leading to the plant. He should then periodically check both the front doors and the bolted doors during his nighttime rounds. He should indicate in his log, first, that the doors are properly secured, and second, whether any of them were later found unlocked or unbolted.

4. In all administrative buildings around the parking lot and in the personnel and security offices, the front door locks should be changed so that there will be one master key for all. This master key should be carried only by the general manager and other persons in the top echelon of management whom he may designate. Another first master will be kept, identified only by number, in a locked cabinet in the security department. A record should be maintained of the issuance of these master keys, and the keys should be die stamped with some symbol to show they were issued by the security department.

5. For each of the administrative buildings there should be a second master key which will open only the front entrance to that particular building. The distribution of these second masters should be to the head of the department in each building and his designated assistants. Again, there should be a written record of the issuance of these keys, signed by the person receiving them. Each key should be die stamped by the security department before issuance.

The master key for each building can also be used to open interior doors in that building. The first master issued to the general manager and his assistants should unlock not only all of the front doors of individual buildings, but also all locked areas in each building. The second master should unlock only the front door to one particular building and locked areas within that building.

6. If employees within individual departments must be able to lock and unlock interior sections of various buildings, they should carry keys which are not master keys. A receipt should be obtained for each of these keys; again, each key

should be die stamped by the security department.

7. All keys to file cabinets and similar locked cabinets within each building can be maintained in a locked key cabinet in that building. Keys to these cabinets should be limited to personnel who open up the buildings in the morning or close them at night. Issuance of the keys to the cabinet should be recorded in a signed receipt. The keys should be die stamped by the security department.

8. No one except the security department should be permitted to make copies of any keys. The security department should obtain all extra keys from the same source and they should be stamped with a distinctive die such as a trademark. A log should be kept in the security department showing signatures of each person assigned a key of any kind. Any keys temporarily assigned should be charged out by the security department and a temporary receipt signed by the person obtaining the key. The temporary receipt should show the time and date the key is returned and should be initialed by the guard to whom the key is turned in.

9. All extra keys should be maintained in the security department in a locked container and should be identified only by number. A list identifying the code numbers by location should be kept locked in a separate place. The key cabinet in the security department should always be kept locked and should not be in a conspicuous location.

10. The code identifying various master keys should be maintained personally by the head of the security department and should not be available to anyone outside of the security department.

Fire Prevention

There has been wide experience in the security field in fire prevention. Training materials and master planning assistance are available from insurance companies and local fire protection organizations. The problem here is not lack of knowledge and experience, but the lack of application of the available experience. Since fires do not happen often, planning to fight them is usually not part of a company's continuing security program.

Regardless of a company's size, it should have a regular schedule of training in fire protection and fire fighting for the security department. Security personnel charged with fire fighting responsibility must have experience fighting actual fires with the plant's fire fighting equipment. If an operation is too small to maintain its own fire fighting equipment on this scale, security staff should be trained to recognize the different types of fires and methods of fighting each one. The local fire department can provide this type of training with its equipment.

A deficiency that shows up in too great a percentage of security surveys is the failure to check and service fire extinguishers on a regular schedule. Fire hoses may have become too rotten to hold water pressure. Hydrants or hose connections may be blocked, locked up or rusted shut. All of these faults come from lack of a positive schedule of fire protection. The company should always act as though the next major fire will happen tomorrow.

Written Job Assignments for Guards

Management is inclined to consider uniformed guards as parasites because part of their activity is static. The presence of uniformed guards at guard stations acts as a deterrent to dishonesty, but because the guards do not look busy, management makes messengers and low-paid servants out of them. They are taken away from true security functions to run errands.

The best way to defeat this is to have written job assignments for each post or station assigned to a uniformed guard. This should be done in any event for good security reasons, but it will also help prevent the errand boy assignments. The orders should be written so they detail the need for security at each post and what losses can occur if each post is not manned. Management can be referred to these orders when a guard is pulled off for messenger work. There are certain irregular functions that will require guards, but even these should be covered by written orders to limit the guards' activity to the required functions.

Joint Efforts for Security

Many retail stores and other small establishments in all business fields recognize the possibility of loss and the need for some kind of security to prevent it. However, because the cost of instituting their own security staff would make them noncompetitive, they accept their losses as part of the cost of doing business.

This is particularly true where a business operates a number of locations spread over a wide area. Convenience grocery stores, filling stations and construction sites are some examples. Each of these types of businesses forms trade associations in order to purchase goods more cheaply, enhance their acceptance by the public, influence legislation, maintain industry standards, and for many other reasons. Each then gains something from the joint effort. The same joint effort could provide the security system for all that none could afford for himself. Enterprises in different fields, but with common security problems, could join together to provide that protection.

For example, contractors could hire watchmen and roving patrols to meet the changing needs for protection at various job sites. Larger retail stores could have a common security force to combat shoplifting. This force could concentrate its efforts for maximum effect for short periods at several stores each day. A concentration of small merchants in one area could provide more policing security for each of them than any one could afford for himself.

Efforts in the past to associate for security reasons have broken down because it was easier to pass the cost of losses on to the consumer than to get together to prevent the losses. But losses now may be approaching the point where the public will reduce its buying rather than pay the high costs. The cost of preventing losses may well be less than the losses themselves. Joint effort can be the first approach to loss prevention.

CASE HISTORY #4

The Arctura Corporation has one parking lot for employees of both plant and office areas. The lot is inside a fenced area but there is no fence between it and either the office or plant.

The plant and office are in the same building. It is inside the fence, except that the front doors of the office are outside the fenced area. Several unsupervised doors lead from the office into the plant. These doors are never locked. There are unsupervised time clock doors from the parking lot into the plant. These are never locked. The doors from the parking lot into the office are never locked.

The single fence gate into the parking area is also used by trucks. One uniformed guard is assigned to the gate during working hours. This gate is locked during non-working hours. Persons driving employees to and from work can drive into the fenced area to get near the plant and office doors.

The padlock on the gate broke recently. The guard was told to buy a new one and get some extra keys made for any employees who might need to get into the plant during non-working hours.

During daylight hours on weekends and holidays there are no guards on duty at the plant. There is one guard on duty inside the plant and office building from 8:00 p.m. until 8:00 a.m. There are no guard clock stations and no assigned duties or guard patrol instructions.

ASSIGNMENT:

List four recommendations for better physical security that you would make in a security survey report of the Arctura Corporation's plant and office, and give your reasons for making them.

Chapter 6

The Security Survey

No problem can be solved until it is identified and understood. Adequate security cannot be planned until a survey establishes what items need protection and how they can best be safeguarded.

A survey is a comprehensive study and examination of an area or problem. Security, as we have defined it, is the state of being secure to the maximum extent that profits will sustain. To attain this maximum feasible level of security, a company must first know the total threat it faces. A security survey attempts to determine the total threat by examining all areas and operations of the facility.

Areas covered by security surveys include various types of physical security and fire protection. While these matters, reviewed in the previous chapter, are an essential part of any security program, they are not the primary subject of this book. The problem we are especially concerned with is employee dishonesty, and the survey will include a search for areas of temptation and the possibilities for dishonest employees to profit from theft.

Who Needs Security Surveys?

A company needs a security survey if it has never before

considered security to be important; if it has a small security department with only limited authority; if it experiences a sudden, substantial and unexplained inventory shortage; or if profits take a sudden, unexplained dip. In other words, if a company needs a great deal more security than it has had in the past and doesn't know how to achieve it, a security survey is called for.

A survey should also be made if a company's present security operations do not produce a reasonable level of employee honesty. If the security department seems poorly directed, lacking in concrete security plans, or outdated — it is time for a security survey.

A survey by an outside security authority will examine what security measures the company has, what it needs and where its major problems are.

Sources of Survey Personnel

A security survey is usually a team effort by two or more people. They should be experienced in security work. As a minimum, one member of the team must have knowledge of plant operations, production matters, and physical security. Another must have knowledge of business forms, accounting and business practices. They will merge their experience and their findings to recommend a security system to match the identified threats.

A company should not use its own production and office personnel for these surveys unless it has an experienced, independent security department. Even then, the survey findings should be tested against outside surveys. These outside surveys can be used to fulfill the role of the "re-survey" discussed later in this chapter.

There are a number of large, national security service organizations which can provide the expertise required to conduct a survey. A company that wants to have a survey made might check among other firms in its field to see whom they have employed for such surveys. In larger cities, there will be local organizations capable of performing surveys. A company may be associated with a larger firm which has a security staff qualified to make a survey, or it may belong to a trade association that can conduct a survey or can recommend a group experienced in that field.

Before choosing a survey source, the company must find out what prior experience the group has had in making surveys. This does not mean that *all* members of the survey team must have made prior surveys, as long as all are experienced in security and follow a detailed survey manual. This manual will have been built up from experience in previous surveys. It will contain check lists for many parts of the survey which can be used by those with no prior survey experience.

The Survey Proposal

A survey is not something tangible that can be measured in quantity or price. It cannot be purchased like a raw material, nor can it be arranged for like the services of a CPA. A survey is not a single package; it is a process that goes through several steps.

First, the decision must be made as to which organization will make the survey. A representative of the survey organization should come to the client's place of business to assess its size and make-up. The client company should then ask for a specific proposal for a preliminary survey only. This proposal should specify the number of men to be employed on the survey, the approximate total man-hours to complete it, and total cost or hourly cost per man. A rate per man-hour, with a limiting total price, is the best method. This allows some variation in total cost. If the company judges during the survey that certain areas or functions need greater emphasis, there is sufficient cost flexibility to allow for that expansion. Conversely, if the survey team places too much emphasis on physical security or some other problem area, the company can vary the survey program to fit its needs more closely.

The preliminary survey report will then be evaluated. Its recommendations will be reviewed to see if any emphasis is misdirected. Will the proposed complete survey be really complete? Will it serve the purpose of prevention of dishonesty? The contract for the complete survey is then made, on the same sort of hourly rate and total price basis.

Preliminary Survey

The preliminary survey serves two purposes:

1. It enables the client company to determine whether the survey group performs adequately.
2. It establishes what will be covered, in what degree, by the complete survey.

The company wants to prevent employee dishonesty, of course. But how is this to be accomplished? Where does it need the most security? What materials are the most tempting to thieves? What items have the highest value after being stolen? These and many other questions will be considered in the preliminary survey. They cannot be completely answered short of a complete survey, but this preliminary review can designate the problem areas and problem materials. It does not set up security procedures. It merely identifies the dangers and makes general recommendations regarding protection.

No complete survey can be conducted properly without this preliminary survey. The survey group needs this opportunity to familiarize themselves with the company and its problems. After this preliminary, fact-finding survey, both the client and the survey group will be in a more informed position when setting the aims and scope of the complete survey.

Setting Survey Goals

No two companies have identical problems. Values of materials differ, crime rates in labor supply areas differ, resulting in varying levels of dishonesty among employees. Buyers of stolen materials are more numerous in large metropolitan areas. Many factors determine the goals of the complete survey. The preliminary survey will indicate where the company is most vulnerable to employee dishonesty. Specific goals can then be set for the complete survey that will provide greatest protection in the areas of greatest risk.

In the final analysis, the client company must decide what the goals of the complete survey should be. The company should not forget, however, that it hired the survey team to find problems and recommend solutions. A competent survey team will make preliminary recommendations for security goals that the client company would not have considered on its own.

Complete Survey

A written schedule of goals should be drawn up as a guide and as a limit for the survey team. This schedule should not be considered a rigid pattern to be followed and should not set priorities for the achievement of goals. There will always be an overlapping of goals; what helps to reach one goal may set up obstacles in achieving another.

Each goal in the survey program should be assigned to one of the client company's executives or supervisors knowledgeable and responsible for that part of the business. The survey team members do not operate in a vacuum. They place themselves in the position of a dishonest employee and look for a gap in security. They have to be sure that the gap does exist and that their solution fills it. A good survey team member will be constantly checking and testing solutions to problems. He needs to confer with someone who knows the problem area involved. The solutions arrived at in this manner will be better and less expensive than those planned without client feedback.

Survey team members should have full access to the plant. Employees should be advised to cooperate fully with the survey team, freely answering all questions put to them. If the company deals extensively with local suppliers, truckers or railroads, the survey team may want to talk to them. The more the survey team knows, the more helpful their report will be to the company.

Tested solutions to problems, referring to each goal set up in the beginning, will be written up in the final survey report. The problems of reaching each goal should be detailed in the report along with action recommended to reach it. If a goal has proven to be unattainable, this should be explained. Each new problem discovered during the survey should be described in detail.

Survey Review

It is not unusual for management at first to consider the survey recommendations excessive and too costly. For this reason, the survey report should be reviewed first, in an entirely technical manner, at the production level. Are the recommendations logical? Will they work? Will they slow production? How much will they cost?

These questions should not be answered merely yes or no. Each recommendation should be answered separately, with the positive and negative sides fully explained. Management will then consider the suggestions in the light of how they will work at the production level. Management should be able to judge whether any negative answers by production people are legitimate or merely represent rejection of suggested change.

The production level review should include the estimated man-hours and dollar cost of putting each suggestion into practice. Management can weigh this information with other factors. If production agrees that certain suggestions are valid, cost little to implement, and will reduce employee dishonesty, then management will be forced to consider these suggestions. Cost will not be the only deciding factor.

This review should consider whether the projected increased security measures will entail one-time costs or continuing expenses. Some suggestions may require only change of a business form, a change in locks or some added duties for a guard. These add little or no continuing cost.

The cost of each suggested change should be considered in the light of its probable effect on employee dishonesty. Will it pay for itself? Some suggestions may seem cost-prohibitive but still need to be followed. A failure to limit dishonesty now may lead to increased future dishonesty that will cost more in the long run.

The moral factor must also be considered. Causing increased honesty in one department pays off in its overall effect on employee honesty. If employees see evidence of security in one area, they will expect it to be present in other areas. Prevention of dishonesty can only strengthen relative honesty.

Thus, management decisions should be based on survey recommendations, plus production level recommendations, plus moral considerations. Cost can only be a consideration when all of these other factors have been weighed. The situation could be likened to a company's decision whether to advertise. Factors known today are combined with projected reaction to future actions (advertising or security measures) to produce a profit that will absorb the cost of the actions.

Recheck Survey

When arrangements are made for a complete survey, the cost should include a recheck survey to be made about six months later. In this period of time the company should have put into effect those parts of the survey suggestions that it accepted. The recheck serves to evaluate the company's understanding of those suggestions. It also lets the survey team check its understanding of its recommendations against the effect of those suggestions on the company's business practices.

The survey team cannot judge any effect on employee dishonesty in this short period of time, but they can see if some adjustments need to be made to improve records flow, to speed production or to ease a morale problem. It is possible that they misunderstood some facet of the business.

They will also check to see whether the company made some change or omission from the suggestions that has reduced expected security. The company may have misunderstood some detail, or implementation of a suggestion may have created a new security problem.

This recheck not only determines how well the company put the plans into effect, but also how good the plans were. It also gives the survey team a chance to evaluate the possible future effects of the company's failure to accept certain recommendations.

The company should consider the survey team's opinions carefully. The survey group has nothing to sell except service; if they do not serve they do not make future sales. The company hired and paid for their expertise, and that experience and knowledge should not be disregarded without good reason. The recheck survey gives both sides a chance to see how reasonable their decisions were.

Periodic Re-Survey

A re-survey once a year is a good idea during the early years of a new or revitalized security department. Security cannot be planned and then forgotten. The security chief may not have the ability to implement a security plan. He may be putting his efforts into uniformed guard service and forgetting other phases of security. He may not really understand good security procedures. His prior experience in this field may be limited. His performance needs to be policed by outside specialists.

A re-survey is also a good idea after major expansion or a product change. The security chief may not fully recognize how these changes affect security patterns.

Even a good security chief will allow small changes in conditions to accumulate until they constitute a major problem. For example, increase in the number of production workers jams available parking areas so that parking overflows into unprotected areas. A new employee entrance gate is opened that is not part of the previously approved employee areas. A food vending machine area is installed where there is no security provided for nearby valuable materials. A periodic re-survey will update the security plan to cover such changes.

Re-surveys will be needed less frequently after the company's security staff gains experience and demonstrated maturity. However, no department should be permitted to police itself. This rule applies especially to the security department. A re-survey every five years or so should be part of the policing of the security department.

Survey Use in Accountability

Section III of this book takes up accountability as a security principle and discusses many specific security procedures. It might seem that a company could simply adopt the systems recommended and dispense with the security survey. However, the proposals presented are only a guide to how accountability works. They are not a chart for any specific business. They are meant only to demonstrate various procedures for protecting a business against dishonest employees. They do not cover all the specific danger points in a particular business.

A security survey, on the other hand, does apply specifically to the particular company. It indicates where dangers are and recommends ways to protect these specific points. As a rule, these recommendations will be in more specific terms than the accountability system outlined in this book.

Accountability is a new approach to the prevention of employee dishonesty. It is a general system, not a cure for spot problems. It can be used in applying security survey recommendations to most types of businesses.

The complete security survey will also aim at protection against outside thieves and many other matters in addition to employee dishonesty. The survey helps to locate all the loss problem areas in a company.

CASE HISTORY #5

The Arctura Corporation's main plant is located in a mid-South city of about 50,000 population. It manufactures electrical and electronic appliances for sale under its own name, and for sale under other national store chain trademarks. It also makes components for use in the finished products of other manufacturers. It has a few branch plants in other parts of the country where it makes such items as plastic parts and shipping cartons for its own use from local raw materials.

Billing, accounting and corporate offices are located in a larger city offering financial facilities not available in the much smaller main plant city.

This corporation has no separate department to handle security matters. Each plant has a few uniformed guards to provide a minimum of security at night, on weekends and holidays when the plants are not operating. The main plant has guards at gates used for receiving raw materials and shipping finished products, for vending machine and utility service trucks, and for related uses. It does not place guards at employee gates.

The guards are employees of the corporation. Most are former production employees who were injured on the job or are too infirm to operate machines. The Captain of the guards at the main plant is a retired police captain who has had no training, other than on-the-job training, either in police work or plant security work. None of the individual guards has ever had training in the use of the firearms they carry. Guards are started at an hourly rate only slightly higher than the legal minimum wage.

There are no written guard manuals or guard post orders.

QUESTIONS

1. Does the Arctura Corporation have adequate security against employee dishonesty?
2. What initial action should the company take to establish adequate security?
3. What are the three general objectives of a security survey?
4. What are the three steps in security surveys?
5. Should a security department be allowed to police itself? State the reasons for your answer.

Section III

ACCOUNTABILITY WHERE IT COUNTS

Chapter 7

Introduction to Accountability

A merchandise loss is compounded by the company's cost in confirming it. Perhaps a greater loss is management's confirmation of its inability to protect its assets. Accountability in a security system requires verification of material counts and personnel information from two or more independent sources. For the system to operate properly, this verification must be made by the security staff. No department can be trusted to police its own functions.

Definitions

Accountability as used conventionally in business means *inventory*. It measures objects or materials that can be seen and counted.

Security accountability as used in this book extends inventory into a flowing system to prevent thefts by employees, to hire relatively honest employees and keep them honest. (Hereafter in this text the term *accountability* will refer only to its use for security purposes.)

A similar term, *accounting*, applies a dollar value to property. Dollar value enters into accountability primarily in determining degree of temptation, or where currency itself is the accountable property to be protected. Otherwise accounting is part of accountability only when it is one of the verifying independent sources.

Business today requires many inventories and quantity reports in its internal system. Present inventory usage has little to do with security functions. Most of these inventories and reports, however, can be used in their present forms in an accountability security system. In this way, security accountability becomes relatively easy to obtain.

Accountability will provide a current and continuous method of counting and verifying materials and information at various danger points. In a manufacturing process, these critical points start with a requisition for materials and end with payment of the sales invoice for the finished product. A system of accountability should be able to prove the quantities purchased, used, used up, stored, sold, and paid for.

Verification of an applicant's relative honesty is as necessary as protection of an employee from the temptation to steal. Accountability in personnel matters begins with the employee application form. Verification of its information assists in the hiring of relatively honest employees. It assists in decisions on promotion and disciplinary actions. It provides the incentive that helps maintain employee honesty.

If material of value is stolen, an accountability system should detect the theft. It should indicate what and how much was stolen. It may also provide the means for identifying all participating employees.

Adapting Accountability Measures

Complete security is not economically feasible; likewise, *complete* accountability is not economical. The examples given in this section will indicate how accountability is established; how it is applied to normal business departments; and under what conditions it is safe and reasonable to reduce complete security to a level that is economically feasible.

The system described here cannot be applied completely and directly to any one business or to all security problems. The model company used in this section is one engaged in general manufacturing. It has all the departments necessary to explain general accountability and how it works for security.

The sample applications of accountability cover problem areas experienced in years of handling security problems in many types of businesses. The reader can select from these suggestions those that apply to his particular business.

The way in which accountability is established is rather simple. The degree to which it is established depends on how secure the company wants to be.

Preventing Large-Scale Thefts

Accountability is not concerned primarily with petty thefts that are limited by the size of an employee's lunch box or coat pocket, or the amount he can throw over the plant fence into the weeds. These smaller thefts and protection against them have been covered in the chapter on "Mechanics of Physical Security."

Accountability is concerned more with preventing thefts in quantities large enough to have commercial value to employees. These thefts are committed for profit, not for personal use. The items are stolen to be sold.

Employees involved in large thefts will seldom see or touch what they steal. To the employee, these thefts seem less like dishonest acts because the thief does not pick up an item and sneak out with it. Employees who would never think of physically taking another person's property will be tempted to commit this type of theft. Taking a kickback from a supplier or shipping a load of finished products without billing the customer are impersonal actions. Temptation comes easier. The feeling of guilt is reduced. This type of theft, however, hurts the employer more because larger quantities are taken.

In some of these larger thefts, there is another factor in addition to profit that cannot be ignored. This is the challenge to an employee to prove he is smarter than the security system. This is often the deciding motive for a disgruntled employee.

Accountability requires that materials which must be

counted be subject to a second count. The second count must be an independent one, taken by other employees or at a different place. It must be compared with the first count to verify whether the employer still has all of his property.

Accountability also requires that statements on employment application forms be verified; that management people be proved to be living within their income; that physical security measures really provide security; and that many things other than materials are verified from a second, unrelated source.

Use of Business Forms

Accountability should use existing records and reports wherever possible. Doing so adds little to costs that can be charged directly to the security department. Most of the counting reports that security will need are already part of normal business procedures, although they are usually prepared for reasons other than security and are not checked against each other. Following is a simple example of what can happen when no accountability system is in effect.

Production fills out a requisition for a specified quantity of items and sends it to the purchasing department. Production hears nothing about its request until the stockroom reports the requisitioned material is received in stock.

The purchasing department received the requisition and issued a purchasing order in the same amount. Suppose, however, that the purchasing agent has an arrangement with the supplier that the order shipped will be short 10 items. The invoice, however, will be for the full quantity ordered.

The receiving department records the actual quantity received. It sends a receiving slip to the purchasing department for 10 items less than the purchase order quantity. The purchasing agent has a pad of blank receiving slips. He makes out a copy showing the quantity as 10 more than was received; he throws away the true receiving slip copy. The false receiving slip copy, with a copy of the purchase order, goes to accounts payable as authorization to pay the invoice. The supplier gets paid for 10 more items than were shipped. The purchasing agent gets a kickback payment.

It couldn't happen to you? Perhaps not in exactly the same way, but it does happen frequently.

An accountability system would have noted that the receiving slip showed a different amount received than ordered. The improper invoices would not have been paid. No new or different forms would be needed to obtain purchasing accountability. Simply a different distribution of purchase order and receiving forms would ensure comparison for accountability.

In Chapter 3, an example was given of a lumber shortage in a large sawmill. The quantity of rough lumber in each log was measured first by the stock pile foreman. This count was used by the tree-cutting crew to keep the stock pile of unsawed logs at a certain level. The rough lumber in each log was measured again by the sawmill foreman for accounting inventory purposes.

In this case, the two records needed by an accountability system were being prepared but never came together for comparison. A slightly different use of the existing reports permitted a clerk to make this comparison and note any difference.

There will be places in some systems where two independent counts are needed but cannot be obtained readily. In any system of production or processing, nearby points can be found where counts are readily available. The distances, or number of steps, between these two points may be small enough for security to make satisfactory comparison. When a security system is "stretched out" this way, however, the company takes a greater risk. Security should take a correspondingly closer interest in places where a greater risk exists.

Numbering and Signing Forms

The reports that are used in accountability should usually be on prenumbered forms. Where possible, they should be signed by the person who makes the count or records the information. Where this is not possible, one copy must bear the signature of the person responsible for the information.

The signing and pre-numbering of the form accomplish two security necessities:

1. The signature records responsibility.
2. Pre-numbering gives security absolute control over each form. No misuse can be hidden.

The last copy of each pre-numbered form will be filed in numerical order in the place where it is prepared. Even if the person who prepares the form signs no other copy, he should sign this one.

Security will inspect each numerical file of these forms each month and will account for each number. *All* copies of each voided form will be filed in this file. This will assure that if the file copy is marked as voided, all other copies are also voided. It should not be possible for one copy to be voided and the other copies used.

In its monthly check of the continuity of this numerical file, security will initial the last number checked. The next month's checking will then start with this initialed copy.

If a number is missing, security will check places where other copies of that form go in normal business use. If all copies are missing, it should be treated as a security problem. If only the numerical file copy is missing, other copies will be checked for possible misuse. A copy should be made to complete the numerical file regardless of any misuse.

Although other copies of these forms will become permanent business records in their normal uses, the files of the last copy of each pre-numbered form are not usually kept as permanent records. The numerically filed copies should be destroyed by security when they are of no further use.

A new numbered series of one of these forms should be identified as a new series. This can be done by preceding the new number series by a letter of the alphabet. All old, unused forms will be picked up by security. There should be no gap in the old forms between the last number used and the first unused one. All old, unused forms should be destroyed by security.

Whenever a new series of forms is adopted, security should verify that the first new series form used bears the correct first number for that series.

If any of these forms are missing from the stock of unused
forms, security should b⸺ ⸺tified at once. Security should put a
⸺ers in the numerical file in proper
⸺nen check places where other copies
⸺th other business records. It should
⸺xists everywhere the form is used or
⸺series starts, a final check should be
⸺ the old forms.
⸺e accountability system where good
⸺her count could be made. It then
⸺e if the security purpose served by
⸺its cost. Will its cost be matched by
⸺produce? After all other factors are
⸺ibility of management not to tempt
⸺ deciding factor.
⸺should try to work around and
⸺procedures and forms. Security
⸺erfering with the normal work flow,
⸺ty levels will permit.

The forms mentioned in this book represent only those
copies required for accountability. The use of these forms places
no limit on the quantities needed for normal business uses.

The following chapters in this section will be titled according to individual business functions. The procedures described
in these chapters will include overlapping use of forms for
accountability, requiring one department's forms to provide
accountability in another department. Instructions on the use of
these forms for accountability will be repeated in other chapters.
Each chapter then will be complete in itself.

The examples given in this section are not patterned after
problems in any one company, nor will they include all possible
accountability measures a company may need. They will merely
show how accountability is obtained, how it operates, and what

it can accomplish. This is a guide, not a pattern.

The problems used as examples have been simplified so that simple accountability solutions can apply. The personnel, purchasing, receiving, fabricating, sales and shipping procedures in an actual company will be much more complicated. The security problems will still be present; their solutions will require adaptations to meet their complexity.

Inform Employees

Whatever the accountability system is, it should be laid out plainly for all employees. A security procedures manual should be prepared showing the overall system: who prepares how many copies of which forms, who gets them, and why.

Employees who will prepare these forms must be told of their individual responsibilities in the system. Each should know what he is required to do and how to do it. He should know that his performance in this area will be checked by the security department.

The company takes a certain risk in informing employees how security measures guard against employee theft. Some employees will use this knowledge to circumvent the system. Many more employees, however, will recognize the risks involved and will be conditioned toward honesty. If the accountability system is made to work, the results will be worth this small risk.

Flexibility Needed

For maximum security, the accountability system must be flexible. The frequency of its checking should increase wherever irregularities are found. Security can make its own verifying counts at points where normal business counts are not made. By its mere presence in making these counts, security increases its conditioning effect.

No security system should ever become routine. No accountability system should rely on always counting the same things at the same places, with the same regularity. Some procedures can be verified on a spot basis at random times. Pressure can be applied when employees become lax. Accountability should indicate where security pressure is needed; security must then apply the pressure.

Summary

Security accountability is a system designed to keep employees honest. An effective accountability program begins with the detailed security survey, which first establishes points where availability and profit combine to tempt an employee to steal. Accountability procedures then provide for the hiring of relatively honest employees and the maintenance of this relative honesty after employment. This is done by a system of verification of information and material quantities by comparison of independent sources. As a rule, these independent sources are already available but are not used for security purposes. When the relatively honest, but tempted, employee sees the high risk of detection created by accountability, he is usually able to resist the temptation.

CASE HISTORY #6

The Arctura Corporation hired outside experts to make a complete security survey. The final survey report is being reviewed by top executives. They find the report very critical of security procedures now being followed; these procedures offer no protection against kickback and diversion schemes by key employees.

The report sets out a broad, complete plan of security accountability. Some of the suggestions in the report deal with the business as a whole, and others apply to specific departments. The executives decide to consider the general recommendations first.

One general problem is that many forms are not numbered until they are prepared. There are no records to show that all numbers of any series are used consecutively, nor that one number is not used more than once. No record is kept of voided numbered forms. A spot check of several different forms showed unexplained gaps in the numbers used.

QUESTIONS

1. Define security accountability.
2. Explain in detail how pre-numbered forms are used in accountability.
3. How should voided forms be accounted for?

Chapter 8

How to Hire
Honest Employees

The personnel department is responsible for obtaining and screening job applicants, but it should not make the final decision on whether to hire an applicant. That decision should rest with someone experienced in the job to be filled. A person at that level is best capable of judging whether the applicant can fill the position.

The personnel department has a second function as a liaison between employees and management in non-job related activities, such as insurance and retirement programs, vacation schedules, social activities, and other matters dealing with morale.

It is the first function, finding and screening job applicants, that is of concern here, since it is the first step in obtaining relatively honest employees.

Job Classification and Standards

In screening a prospective employee, the personnel department should verify that the applicant has the education, ability or experience the job requires. Personnel must know exactly what job is open and what levels of skills and experience are required to fill it. Jobs should be classified and standards set for each level of classification. The *size* of the operation will have little to do with these divisions; the *type* of business will govern the primary job classifications. The classifications will define general job types, such as shipping clerk, punch press operator, stenographer, janitor, etc.

Each classified group will be broken down further into various levels of proficiency and experience. Here the *size* of the business will determine the extent of the breakdown. A "stenographer" may be an executive secretary, a steno pool employee, or a receptionist who does only enough transcribing to keep busy in the reception room.

There will be many overlapping duties in some jobs, such as the stenographer/receptionist. This will require some arbitrary subdivisions of classifications. These divisions should be made according to who supervises that job classification. If the stenographer is the supervisor for this job because of the technical skill it requires, then this classification will be a subdivision of stenography. If, on the other hand, the office manager supervises this position because little or no stenographic skill is required, then the classification will be a subdivision of functions under the office manager.

Stenographers using shorthand or stenotype machines, for example, should all be under one supervisor because the hiring decisions will depend on proof of proficiency in those fields. A receptionist who transcribes machine-recorded dictation will still need to be tested on the related typing skill. Each required skill test should be given by one supervisor so that each applicant being tested for that job skill receives the test in the same way. Tests must be job-related, and they must be provably uniform for all applicants.

As another example, a person who types bills of lading will need to be reasonably proficient in typing, but need not pass a speed typing test. It is more important that this employee be familiar with business forms and shipping procedures. Therefore a supervisor experienced in business forms and shipping should make the final hiring decision for this position.

Job standards will follow the same general classification scheme. For example, general requirements will be set as to experience and minimum physical ability for a "punch press operator." Some positions in this category will also require prior experience on a particular complex machine. Automated machines require another specific skill. The subdivisions of job standards should be exact enough so that the applicant does not waste his and the employer's time applying for a job for which he is not qualified. When the personnel department receives an order for a particular type of employee, they should know exactly what to look for in applications, and the applicants should know whether they qualify before they fill out the application form.

Government Regulations on Hiring

Most employers are familiar with Title VII of the Equal Employment Opportunity Act. Since March 24, 1973, the EEO Commission has jurisdiction over all employers of 15 or more persons. Recent amendments have given the Commission authority to go to U.S. District Court for enforcement of an order against discrimination.

Each company's personnel department should be on the mailing list for the EEOC Field Office in its area. One person in the personnel department must keep up-to-date on changing regulations and required reports. Many employers' problems with EEOC stem from lack of knowledge about minor regulation changes. The frequency of these changes makes it impossible to cover the regulations in detail in this book.

There are a few general points applying to employee dishonesty which can be mentioned. An applicant's prior criminal record is one instance. An employer cannot refuse to hire someone based on arrest records alone; the record must show convictions, recent enough to cause reasonable belief in present dishonesty.

A polygraph test is the best method for determining present dishonesty levels. These tests must be given uniformly to all applicants considered for employment in high temptation areas. The employer can decide which job classifications require polygraph tests, where legally permitted, but it cannot limit the test to some of the acceptable applicants for that classification.

There are other legitimate factors that may eliminate an applicant from consideration: for example, lack of required experience; incomplete application form; false information on the form. These eliminations should be made before polygraph testing of the remaining applicants. Polygraph examination will be covered in more detail later in this chapter.

An employer need not retain an incompetent employee simply because he is a member of a minority group. Retaining such an employee creates a morale problem among other workers who know he is incompetent. Resentment among the other employees may reduce their acceptance of competent minority group employees.

The most important guideline of Title VII is that *there shall be no disparity or unequal treatment in selecting or hiring applicants because of their race, color, religion, age, sex or national origin.*

APPLICATION FORMS

Many companies in the past have merely adopted the employment application form used by some other company, giving little thought to its content or the uses to be made of the information requested on the form. The Equal Employment Opportunity Act and its resulting regulations have caused companies to reappraise their employment applications. The Act forbids employers to ask an applicant for information on his race, color, religion, sex or national origin. Good judgment should also cause many other application form changes.

There are two unrelated reasons for application forms:

1. To obtain statistical information.
2. To obtain job-related information.

Separate forms should be used to obtain each type of information. Both forms should be on letter size paper for easy handling by applicants. There should be ample space for hand-written answers to encourage complete information.

Statistical Forms

The statistical form should ask only for information needed for payroll, Social Security, credit union, insurance, retirement and other non-job uses.

In general the statistical form will ask for the following:

Application date
Full name of applicant
Present address
Telephone number
Date of birth
Social Security number
Name and phone number of person to be notified in emergency
Married or single
Number of minor children and dependent adults
Number of income tax deductions desired

This is not intended to be a complete list. Various other items will be required depending on state and local regulations. Job-related data should not be included on this form.

The statistical form permits the first check on the applicant's relative honesty. The applicant should be checked against the company's own file of former employees not subject to re-hire. The name, date of birth, address and Social Security number are sufficient for identification in local credit and criminal files.

This form should be the same for all applicants. Each applicant should fill out this form first. It can then be indexed and held pending consideration of the applicant for employment. If there are more acceptable applicants than job openings, the employer may wish to hold some applications for later consideration. If this is the case, it is best to renew the statistical information at the time the applicant is reconsidered. The data should not be considered current if it is more than 60 days old.

Job-Related Forms

The job-related form will require different information for different job classifications. It will be simpler for the applicant and more informative for the employer if separate forms are prepared for each job classification.

Each job-related form should begin by identifying the job classification. Next should be spaces for the applicant to repeat some data that will match this form positively with the statistical form. This need only be:

Application date
Name of applicant
Date of birth
Social Security number

These can be put on two lines at the top of the form. This much of each job-related form will be identical. Beyond this there are two rules that govern what information is requested:

1. Only information related to the specific job classification should be asked for.
2. Only information that the company intends to verify should be asked for.

Traditionally, all application forms asked routinely for complete education details. Some jobs were limited to persons with high school diplomas. Employers refused to consider any applicant unless he listed a high school diploma, but they never checked the high school for verification.

A high school diploma in itself qualifies no one for a job. If the job requires some reading ability, the applicant should be tested for his ability to read and understand the material he will need to perform that job. If the job requires typing, he should be tested for his ability to type the sort of material required in that job. If the job requires stenographic ability, the applicant should be tested for speed and spelling ability. If the job requires technical knowledge, he should be asked for places, date and length of education in that field. These sources should be checked for verification. If the job requires only manual dexterity, an advanced education will not increase an applicant's ability to perform that job.

Many application forms ask for references, names and addresses of relatives, and much more information not related to the job being filled. If information is not going to be used, it should not be included on the form.

Application forms often ask for job-related information that the employer has no intention of verifying. Very few application forms are filled out with complete honesty. Relative honesty is one of the most important considerations in choosing an applicant for employment. For that reason alone the information on the employment form should be verified.

Most employers accept the applicant's answers about places and dates of prior employment without checking. Length and dates of employment are the two things most often falsified on applications, and this information should be verified.

One example will illustrate a number of reasons for requiring verification. A man applied for a job requiring a high level of education and experience. The position required excellent knowledge of the subject in order to make convincing presentations to high level executives. None of the information the applicant included on his form was verified. The company assumed he was qualified because his application form said he was qualified.

A few months after being employed, the man ran for the top office in a civic club. One of his opponents in the election did some checking on his background and brought the results to the employer. An investigator was then asked to verify all the information on the employee's application form. He had listed a night school law degree from a college that gave no night law courses in the years stated. He listed attendance at a prestigious university which had no record of him. He had inflated the salary paid him in two prior jobs. His termination date on one job and starting date on the next job indicated he had gone directly from one to the other. Investigation indicated there was actually a gap of about six months, during which time he held a job not listed on the application form. He had been discharged from this job for good reason.

He had built up his spurious background and experience on applications he had filled out for his last three jobs. He had systematically lied so that the difference between succeeding application forms was not great. The difference between any of these forms and reality, however, was very real and pertinent.

If an applicant's background, training or experience are important to his ability to do the required work, this information should be included on the application. The data on the form should serve only as a path to a source which can verify it. In seeking relatively honest employees, the company cannot accept the applicant's evaluation of his own honesty.

Information Sheet

The information on the statistical and job-related forms will be more complete if the applicant understands the reasons for all questions. This is best accomplished by an information sheet which the applicant should read before filling out either form.

The information sheet should be divided into statistical and job-related sections. Each section should follow the same order as the questions on the forms, explaining why the questions are asked and what type and how much information is required in the answers.

Since the same statistical form is used for all applicants, this part of the information sheet can be the same as well. Since the job-related form is different for differing job classifications, however, various information sheets will be needed. The information sheet instructions can enable the employer to use one classification application for several jobs within that category. The applicant can be told which numbered questions to answer for the specific job he is applying for, and which questions he should ignore. For example, one application form could cover all clerical jobs. Instructions would tell a typist or a stenographer which questions to answer.

This is not as complicated as it sounds if the employer asks only for job-related information that it intends to verify. There is an added factor here that affects hiring costs: an informed applicant will provide more complete information that allows the hiring supervisor to make a more informed decision.

The information sheet can be simplified by putting the statistical instructions (which are the same for all jobs) on one side and the job-related information on the reverse. Thus only one side must be varied for different job classifications.

The job-related section of the instructions can, if space permits, describe the various job levels available in each classification. This is a good opportunity to explain how an employee can progress to better-paying jobs.

The primary purpose of the information sheet is to inform the applicant what he needs to include in his application to give the employer the fullest required information. The completed form provides the first step in the hire/no-hire decision.

The information sheet should warn the applicant to give only truthful answers on all forms. He needs to know that he will not be considered for employment if he gives false information. He should be told that all his answers will be verified as to honesty and completeness.

No-Hire Decisions and Documentation

There will generally be more applicants than job vacancies for most non-technical jobs. Some acceptable applicants will not be hired. Those application forms retained for later consideration should be used within a stated, limited time. Verified information over 60 days old needs to be re-verified before employment. Credit, criminal and employment information can change materially in a 60-day period.

Application forms showing some deficiency in required ability, or where investigation has produced evidence of falsified information, should be retained as proof of reason for non-hire. The reasons for non-hire must be recorded in such detail that they can be proved in court. The legal protection afforded applicants today puts the burden of proof on the employer. The employer should be sure it can provide a legal reason for non-hire.

A company's experience with EEOC and additional local requirements will determine how long it retains all non-hire application forms in its files. This will be discussed further under the heading "Applicant Indexing."

Obvious job-related deficiencies or proven dishonesty in filling out the forms will permit the personnel department to make some no-hire decisions. A decision to hire should come only after an interview by the hiring supervisor. The experienced supervisor may weed out some applicants by comparison of verified job-related information before interview, but he should not hire based on this information alone. The final interview can be much more informative than any application form.

The applicant's race, color, sex, religion and national origin are not known by the hiring supervisor up to the time of the interview. The hiring supervisor must be very sure that his non-hire decision cannot be shown to be based on any of these factors. Non-hire decisions should be well documented.

Applicant Certifications

An applicant is offering himself for hire when he fills out the application. The hiring company has the right to set specifications of ability and experience that will tell the applicant whether he is qualified for the job opening. Most applicants will not waste their time applying for jobs they know they cannot handle. The employer can also set limitations that are not job-connected. For example, he may not want to hire relatives of present employees; or he may give physically handicapped persons preference in plant areas which are easily accessible.

The information sheet given to each applicant helps him understand the job requirements and assists him in filling out the application. The sheet, however, can only be helpful to those who have read it. The last paragraph of the information sheet should be a certification, signed by the applicant, that he has read and understands the instructions. If two sides of the sheet are used, the certification should state that the applicant has read both sides.

The statistical and job-related forms should both include a signed certification that all information furnished by the applicant is truthful. This should include a statement that untruthfulness discovered before hiring will prevent hiring, and untruthfulness discovered after hiring can be sufficient cause for discharge. Acknowledgement of this by the applicant before hiring becomes as much a part of the hiring conditions as work experience. A prospective applicant who has something to hide will be induced not to apply. The company's stated intention to verify all information on the application should not be an idle threat; the employer should not depend on the threat to take the place of verification.

Certification of the job-related application form can contain any special certifications required by the job. If the job is one of high temptation, polygraph tests may be required of all applicants. The certification should then contain an agreement by the applicant to pass a polygraph test before being hired and to be retested at stated intervals if hired. If the job requires a special license or passage of a proficiency test, that should also be stated as a condition for hiring and retention of job.

These certifications allow the employer to set job standards as part of the hiring contract. The prospective applicant then knows the standards before applying. He agrees that he is liable for punitive action if he violates those standards. These certifications are very important to the success of the company's efforts to hire relatively honest employees. Their use also gives the employer a measure of authority to discharge employees whose lies on application forms are not discovered until after hiring.

Honesty certifications should be standard on all application forms. The applicant should always certify that he has read and understood all instructions. Certifications can go as far beyond these matters as security and reason suggest for the job to be filled. This is a main line of defense against dishonest employees. It costs nothing and should be used to its full capacity.

Applicant Indexing

An index card should be prepared and filed for each person who fills out an application form. It need not contain much information. For purely identification purposes it should include:

Name
Address
Date of birth
Social Security number
Date of application

It can also contain a space to check "hired/non-hired." If the statistical application form is kept as a permanent record, the index card information may be reduced to:

Name
Social Security number
Hired
Terminated
Non-hired

The indication of whether the applicant was hired and whether he is still employed refers the employer to active or inactive personnel files if further information is needed.

The personnel department should check the card file for each new applicant to determine whether he has been considered for employment in the past. Prior information may help in the evaluation of the present application. Any applicant investigation should include comparison of prior application information with verified current information. Rehiring will depend in part on length of former employment and reason for termination.

APPLICANT INVESTIGATIONS

Every applicant must furnish certain basic information. As we have stressed, all of this must be verified before he is hired.

Some of it can be verified at the time the application is filled out. The name can be verified from a driver's license. The address can be verified from a city or telephone directory, from credit files, or, as a last resort, from an open neighborhood inquiry. Date of birth will appear on voter registration records, some driver's licenses, credit records or school records. Social Security cards should be produced when the application is filled out.

Credit Checks

Local credit information sources should be checked for all applicants considered for employment. Some restrictions are being placed on dissemination of this type of information. The no-hire decision should not be based on credit information unless the credit source will furnish the employer a written report, or unless the verbal report is verified from other sources.

An occasional slow pay report is not important in itself. Indicators to look for include defaults, judgments, repossessions and personal bankruptcies. Two other signs of instability have a relationship to relative honesty:

1. Habitual borrowing from more than one personal finance company.
2. Monthly loan and time payments equal to more than half the applicant's monthly earnings.

A person who has borrowed from two personal loan companies at the same time has almost certainly not told one of them the truth about his unpledged assets. A person paying out over 50% of his income in time payments needs another source of income to meet these obligations. A second job can reduce his effectiveness and performance as an employee. Or his additional income may come from thefts from his employer.

A poor credit rating must be judged in the light of recent information. Many young people get into heavy debt because of lack of experience and easy access to credit. The record of the most recent two or three years should be checked to see if they have learned from their experience.

Too much continual debt without a reasonable emergency need indicates susceptibility to temptation and a lack of judgment that should influence the hiring decision. The no-hire decision, however, should not be based on unverified credit information showing overextension only. The decision should be based on verified information.

Criminal Records Checks

Every applicant considered for employment should be checked for a local criminal record. EEOC states that an employer cannot refuse to hire an applicant with multiple arrests who has never been convicted. If those arrests involved theft of property, the employer should determine why none of them resulted in convictions. In the case of recent arrests, final action may not yet have been taken on the case.

A clear record for five years following one or more convictions might indicate that experience has caused a change in attitude. Recent uncleared theft arrests of an applicant should automatically cause the employer to choose another satisfactory applicant. An employee inclined toward stealing can always find something of his employer's to steal. No hard rule can be set for judging a person's criminal record. Cost of complete investigation is usually prohibitive.

Work Experience Verification

Certain jobs call for skills which cannot be measured adequately by a proficiency test and must be evaluated by the applicant's past experience. Examples include a crane operator, purchasing agent, paint mixer, shipping clerk, sawmill foreman, and hundreds of other jobs. The employer must verify the applicant's type and length of experience. How much information the employer demands depends on the importance of the particular job.

This information should be verified in person rather than relying on correspondence. Former employers will be more candid in personal contact than in written communication. A letter addressed to a former employer will usually be answered by the personnel department without divulging anything first-hand about the applicant.

Who Should Investigate?

The company's own security employees should make applicant investigations in the local area on all applicants below executive level. There are private investigative groups of national scope who can obtain applicant information across the country. The local sheriff or police department will know law enforcement officers in other areas who can be contacted to obtain information during off-duty hours. There are also former Special Agents of the FBI doing investigative work in many parts of the country.

The local verification should be completed before undertaking the expense of a distant investigation. Although it is easy to take a chance on an applicant rather than pay for an investigation, this is not wise or economical in the long run. A dishonest person who can no longer obtain local employment has only to move 200 miles away to start a new dishonest work record. It costs money to hire, train and discharge a dishonest employee and to replace what he stole. It is cheaper to verify the information on application forms, establish past honesty and competence, and obtain years of productive work from the employee.

Polygraph Examination

In some positions the employee has greater access to valuable materials or to methods of diverting purchases or sales for his own profits. In these positions of greatest vulnerability the polygraph can be used to establish relative honesty before hiring an applicant. Accountability will then help to maintain that degree of relative honesty.

The polygraph establishes the truth of answers to pertinent questions. It can establish whether the person tested has stolen anything in a given period of time; the value of anything stolen; whether the theft was from an employer; and whether he intends to steal from his employer if hired. The questions should be standardized for all applicants and must be related to the job involved. The examination should be limited to determining immediate past and present honesty as it relates to employment. The employer should make sure the applicant has signed the application certifying his agreement to take the test.

If employees are faced with constant temptation and easy access to goods or cash, it may be necessary to give them regular polygraph tests at stated intervals as a deterrent factor. This should also be understood before employment.

It should be noted that some states have passed laws severely limiting the use of polygraph in most employment situations. Legal advice should be sought before instituting a polygraph testing program.

HIRED EMPLOYEE POLICIES

Terms of Employment

As already discussed, certain terms of employment are made clear to the applicant at the time he fills out his employment application. Other terms of employment apply after the applicant has been hired. These are not directly applicable to honesty or dishonesty, but they do indicate a level of moral responsibility that reflects an employee's level of relative honesty.

After an applicant is hired he must work at certain levels of productivity to justify his pay. His total employment activity must be profit-productive. He must arrive in his work area by a prescribed time. Being tardy a certain number of times in a stated period should be sufficient basis for discharge. Missing a certain number of days' work during a stated period should result in an investigation to determine the reason. Discharge should result if the reason is not valid.

Tardiness and absenteeism are often related. In one company where employees were often late or absent, examination of time card records showed that most absences followed a pattern — certain employees were always late or absent on a particular day of the week. Outside investigation showed that these employees held second jobs. Some were bartenders; some drove taxis; some were relief security guards in other plants. One was a deputy sheriff who got part of his night's sleep on his tour of duty.

Some employees should be restricted to certain plant areas. A receiving clerk, for example, must be on hand when material is received. A gate guard is of no value away from his post. A telephone operator is working only when answering the telephone.

All employees are more productive if allowed reasonable breaks from their jobs. These breaks should be closely controlled so that one idle employee does not cause an extra heavy workload on fellow employees. The inconvenience to fellow workers sometimes causes poor work production; it always causes lower morale.

Standards for Termination

There should be written standards warning employees against those habits that cause lower production and poor morale. The employees should know what is expected of them and the consequences of failure to maintain those standards. Punitive actions should be stated for various levels of violations. Some violations will be cause for termination. This should be stated specifically. Definite knowledge of specific punishment is a strong deterrent against improper behavior.

Each new employee should sign an acceptance of these terms of employment as a final step in the hiring process. His signature should be witnessed by the hiring supervisor. The form then becomes a permanent part of his personnel file.

Terms of employment and termination procedures will vary from company to company. In all cases, standard procedures should be set up. Any deviation or variation could prompt a charge of an equal opportunity violation, resulting in expensive legal action.

Employee Personnel Files

Present federal and local employment regulations require very complete personnel files. Possible charges of discrimination in hiring or discharging make it important to maintain the personnel file for a long period after an employee is terminated. The files also assist in providing references to subsequent employers.

Personnel files begin with the signed applicant instruction sheet, the statistical application form and the job-related form. There should also be an evaluation report by the hiring supervisor and the signed terms-of-employment form. This is the basic employee personnel file. It will thereafter acquire various statistical information changes and other changes dealing with retirement and insurance plans, etc.

A certain amount of employee turnover is inevitable. The rate will vary depending on many factors unrelated to employee honesty.

An employee who remains on the job for one year should be considered worthy of consideration for advancement in pay scale and job classification. This is an arbitrary period considered by most employers as the maximum time which should elapse before each re-evaluation. The evaluation should be made in written form by a supervisor of the employee. Each employee should read and initial his report. His initialing indicates only that he has read it, not necessarily that he approves the report. These reports then become part of the personnel file.

The personnel file should be a running source of information on an employee's abilities, attitudes and performance. Good reports can be rewarded. Bad reports can contain the basis for later punitive action. Reports of all such actions should be included in the personnel files. These reports will provide documented information which can result in promotion or discharge. Promotions are then more likely to come from ability and performance than from favoritism; discharges will be based on defensible reasons.

The evaluation reports serve another useful service: statistical information can be updated at the same time.

Employee Promotions

Employee promotion is a positive contribution toward better morale, a more responsible job attitude, better company loyalty and higher relative honesty.

A raise in pay is not really a promotion. It results more often from length of job tenure. The employee does not consider it a promotion. Being moved to a better job with more pay is a promotion; being given supervision over others, with more pay, is a promotion. Promotions usually reinforce the promoted employee's honesty. He is motivated to keep his new position.

The morale and relative honesty of other employees can also be affected by promotions. The effect is beneficial if fellow workers accept the promotion as a well-earned one. If employees see promotions resulting from favoritism rather than merit, the effect is negative. Promotions must be made for sound reasons. They are best made after consultation between the employee's supervisor and the next higher level of supervision.

Morale can also be hurt if an outsider is brought in to fill a supervisory job when the employees feel one of them should have been promoted to it. Employee feelings are not a primary factor in such decisions, but if everything else is about equal, the company saves money and helps morale by promotion from within its own ranks.

Temporary Employees

Providing temporary employees has become a widespread, competitive service industry. Skilled and unskilled temporary employees are available, but the greatest demand is for unskilled laborers. It is more economical for an employer to use the temporary employment agency than to find and hire people willing to work part-time when needed. Under some temporary employee hiring plans, the employer never knows the identity of these persons. They are treated almost as non-people.

Temporary employees should be considered security risks merely because the employer does not know them and their relative honesty. Their working areas should be as confined as possible. They should not be allowed the same freedom of movement as regular employees. They should not be given keys to any high-security areas. Their work should be supervised and security staff should check them into and off the premises to be sure none remain behind.

Most temporary employees are honest, of course; but their relative honesty is likely to be lower than that of full-time employees. Temporary agencies do little or no background investigation of the employees they provide. The employer does not check their background as in the case of full-time employees. The company must recognize the greater risk and protect itself against it.

CASE HISTORY #7

The security survey conducted for the Arctura Corporation recommended a complete revamping of activity and aims of the personnel department. At the present time this department deals only with plant personnel hiring. The office manager finds and hires all office personnel. The personnel department merely records these employees after they are hired.

The Arctura Corporation uses one application form for all employees, regardless of job classification. The legal size application form was copied ten years ago from one used by the employment manager in a prior job. It contains one line to record the applicant's race and another to record his religion. It also asks for three non-relative references and a listing of all prior employment with only the years of such employment required. No skill-related tests are given. The personnel department bases the employment decision on a review of the application and an interview in the personnel department.

In a pending court case, the Arctura Corporation has been charged with discharging a stenographer for reasons of race and color. This employee had stated on her application form that she had a high school diploma and could type 60 words a minute. After employment her typed letters showed many uncorrected typing errors, misspelled words, and poor knowledge of business terms. She responded to all criticism by claiming racial discrimination on the part of her supervisor. She was verbally discharged, and no written record was kept of her poor work production.

QUESTIONS

1. What changes in the practices of the personnel department should the survey have recommended regarding:
    (a) Make-up of the application form?
    (b) Decision to hire employees?
    (c) Clerical applicant tests?
2. How could Arctura Corporation protect itself from allegations such as those made by the discharge stenographer?

Chapter 9

Executive Accountability

An executive requires the ability and skill to manage and direct the affairs of others. A primary part of this capacity to manage is the ability to maintain the relative honesty of his employees. He must, therefore, be at least as honest as the goal he sets for those employed under him. His personal integrity sets an example.

Each executive represents a large investment by the company in its future, and the company should protect this investment. Security controls over the executive's performance should be strong enough to guarantee his continued honesty.

What Is An Executive?

An executive breathes life into the company's master plan. He may be told to manufacture a product for a certain cost. To accomplish this he has to consider raw materials, production machines and personnel. One of the executives under him will handle purchasing. The purchasing executive will be told to buy certain materials within certain price limits for a specific production level. The purchasing executive finds sources, arranges delivery schedules and methods, and arranges storage facilities at the plant.

Executives create the plans for the repetitive actions that will be carried out by supervisors and foremen at the production level. The executive decides what must be done and how it is to be done. The foreman merely sees that these decisions are carried out.

The executive is the connecting link between the company's master plan and its production line; between the master plan and the selling of the product; between the master plan and the finances needed to carry it out.

Executive Responsibilities

The duties of an individual executive are not quite as sharply fixed as defined above. He helps to formulate the plans he will carry out, and he finds the means for doing so. He then makes sure they are carried out on a day-to-day basis. He meets with the top executive staff one day and solves a labor problem on the production floor the next day.

In another sense the foreman keeps production running smoothly while the executive makes sure it runs on a profitable basis. The executive goes beyond production to consider product image, public relations, cost and corporate financing.

A person promoted from a supervisory job to an executive position must change the direction of his job attitudes. In the past the quantity and quality of his production (or the production of those he supervised) determined his earning power. He was not concerned with the cost of the raw materials or the price charged for the finished product.

As an executive he must be able to instill his former attitude in foremen and workers under him, while his own self interest now begins to change direction. Now he must consider how production can make a *profit*. He is no longer merely making something to sell for money to pay his wages. He now enters the area where money from sales of the product must also pay dividends and taxes, provide for new equipment, and encourage bankers to lend money. He must recognize that profit is as important as product.

The supervisor's ability to make this change in attitude will be one of the early indications of his executive capacity.

As an executive is promoted to higher levels, he must become more profit-oriented. He must begin to delegate individual production and marketing problems to subordinate executives for solution. He now considers general production and marketing problems from the viewpoint of their impact on profits. His decisions must consider the desires of directors and stockholders.

Executive Security Problems

This need to change attitude sometimes creates a stress factor that becomes a security problem. Some men with good technical skill cannot adopt executive thinking. They cannot see profits as the incentive that provides money for production. These people seldom progress beyond the lower levels of executives. If they are permitted to stay in those low level jobs, the company soon finds that most of its low level executive positions are filled by this type of employee. They are merely another level of foremen, where executives are needed. They will be dissatisfied employees, generally infecting others with their dissatisfaction. Many kickback situations start at this level, as the conniving supplier looks for the misfit junior executive.

The most serious executive security problems occur when the head of a corporation forgets his responsibilities to the stockholders and directors and uses his corporate position for his own advantage. He considers the company and its assets his personal property.

Example: A national corporation had its financial headquarters in New York, with operating branches in scattered large cities. Original bookkeeping entries were made at each branch for that branch's operations. New York received summary accounting information and prepared all financial statements. The top executive officer operated one of these branches and lived in its city.

This officer bought some undeveloped land for himself. He

used company personnel and materials to improve and develop the land, charging the expense to various company jobs. When completed, the property was worth over $250,000. It had cost him only about one-tenth that amount. The corporation paid for the balance.

There was no control of executive honesty here. This executive had a history of this attitude toward ownership of company property. He should never have been allowed to reach the executive level where he could cause so great a loss.

Each step up the executive ladder increases the executive's power and the temptations toward dishonesty. An executive is better able to circumvent controls than are rank-and-file employees, because he himself operates some of those controls. His greater knowledge of the business opens new opportunities for dishonest activity. Pricing factors, customers' names, future business plans and new product designs are known to him. All of these are worth money to a competitor.

Varying Levels of Executives

No general description identifies all executive duties, and no form of executive security will cover all executive positions. In examples in this chapter and elsewhere in this book, a large diverse manufacturing plant is used to explain a security system. This permits application of general rules to varying executive levels.

A company operating a series of small manufacturing plants has the same general security problems as a large central plant, and it must apply the same executive security procedures. Although it may have only two executive levels in each widely separated location, this shallow executive depth should not lead the company to ignore executive security. The distance of branch locations from central office security is an added inducement toward dishonesty.

The owner of a small business may have only one executive between himself and production. He should remember that this one executive is subject to all the temptations and opportunities that would be faced by a number of executives in a larger organization.

Small branches in isolated locations may have only one executive at each location. The authority he exercises, and his isolation, will make him extremely vulnerable to temptation.

The type and size of the establishment does not remove the need for executive security. It merely changes the degree of its application.

Choosing Executives

Whether promoted from the ranks or newly hired, an executive must be relatively honest *at that time.* His future must be circumscribed by controls that make most temptations toward dishonesty impractical or unprofitable. These controls will include the general ones discussed in other chapters on accountability, reinforced by others applicable only to executive status. These will be more personally restrictive than those required for production employees or foremen. A man considered for executive status must be able to live and work within these personal restrictive controls.

Those choosing future executives should consider emotional stability as a primary requisite. All other abilities fail if added executive stresses cause impulsive decision-making, if emotional instability creates confusion or disharmony among those working under the executive, or if emotional stress leads to moral deterioration.

An executive must have some ability to control other people in a constructive way. Lack of this ability causes a great turnover in first-level executives. Popularity alone is not enough. The new executive must be able to manage others so they perform their work more efficiently.

At lower executive levels technical proficiency in any one management field is not as important as the ability to gain technical proficiency wherever assigned. Some men will only progress in narrow fields of their own choice. For example, they may become extremely proficient executives in accounting and finance but show no interest or ability in marketing. They will be good executives in their chosen areas but have no interest in higher executive level jobs.

This narrowing of executive vision can be a good thing if done voluntarily. Not all junior executives can be promoted to higher levels; succeeding higher levels require fewer executives. Voluntary specialization can lead to extraordinary proficiency in lower executive positions. This proficiency is its own reward to those executives. Danger comes when a junior executive fails to progress because of lack of ability. Where he wants to progress but cannot keep pace with those better qualified, he sours on his work. His judgment lessens as a moral influence, and temptation finds an easy foothold.

Thus the proper personality, ability and desire to learn are important attributes for the executive. Education in management fields can indicate a person's desire and ability to learn, but the executive's personality can only be judged finally from his use of executive power and the way he learns from executive experience. He can gain this experience within one company, or the company can hire someone who has gained experience under other employers. Either way, on-the-job experience is necessary for a final decision on executive potential. This is bound to cause a rather high turnover among low level executives.

Since a company will probably hire some junior executives from other employers at times, it can expect that other employers will likewise hire away some of its junior executives. Because of this expected turnover, the employer should always be on the lookout for foremen and supervisors in its own plant who show executive potential. The company should be sure as well that it does not hire its competitors' junior executives with emotional problems.

Disclosure vs. Right to Privacy

Some people considered for executive promotion will regard any security investigation into their background as an infringement of their right to privacy. However, earning a living can never be a completely private matter. Once a person enters the employment marketplace, he leaves some privacy behind.

When a person supervises the work of others in a profit-making enterprise, he leaves the private sector of the individual worker. His private life and habits will influence his attitudes toward those he supervises and will have a bearing on his success as an executive. His habits and attitudes must be known to his superiors. An executive should realize that, in order to judge how he will perform, the company must learn about his habits and life style. The higher his position and authority and the greater his responsibility to the owners, the more they must know about him.

The executive may be responsible only to a one-man company owner, but if that owner borrows money from a bank, the executive's responsibilities then spread to the lender. If a corporation's stock is widely held, the executive's responsibility can be nationwide. The higher a person goes in executive positions, the more public his life becomes. Executive security and public confidence require that he leave some privacy behind when he becomes an executive. The man who cannot understand the reasons for this sacrifice of privacy should not be considered for higher executive positions.

The initial response of most new executives to the need for personal disclosure will be negative. Part of the training for executive status should cover the reasons for these disclosures. Those who have real executive capacity and desire will understand the public nature of the job. They will accept the disclosure of private information as part of the price they pay for advancement.

The rest of this chapter will deal with the types of private information that executives must provide, and how these are used in an executive security system.

Executive Personnel Files

A standard statistical job application form will be filled out by all applicants in all job classifications. Employees being promoted to executive status will have filled one out already. Newly hired executives will have filled one out when considered for hiring. This is a standard form that the personnel department will retain for payroll and related uses. A photocopy of this form will be the first item placed in a new personnel file for each new executive.

This executive personnel file will not be prepared for, nor retained by, the personnel department. Executive personnel files will be confidential because of the type of personal information each executive will be required to furnish. These files will be retained in the offices of the highest executive who supervises the new executive. The file's contents must be protected so that those who provide the information will not fear publication.

The confidential information which each executive will be required to furnish when hired or promoted to executive status will be in two categories. The first will deal with financial information. The second will cover organizations and personal associates.

The same information will be required again of all executives promoted to higher executive positions, and at stated periods other than promotions. The period between submissions will vary from company to company as the necessity for security varies; it should not be longer than five years in any case.

Resubmissions are needed for comparison with prior submissions. A special submission may be called for where information is received that an executive is heavily in debt or is living beyond his income. Executives should be advised that some parts of this information will be checked. This will generally be limited to information from public or normal business sources. Executives should also be told that any unusual circumstances can cause further confidential inquiry. They should also be told that providing materially false information can be cause for punitive action.

Executive personnel files will also contain other reports obtained regularly and with greater frequency. Each executive should be rated once a year by his superior and by each higher level that is familiar with his work. An annual credit report should be obtained from the local credit bureau. Derogatory reports from any sources should be filed here also, along with results of investigation of any such reports. Any suggestions made by an executive should be filed in his personnel file with comments on their merit.

The personnel file will be a complete work history and personal history of all matters dealing with the activity and ability of each executive. Each executive should be permitted to review his personnel file as he feels he needs to do so. Each piece of derogatory information should be brought to his attention after any investigation is completed. He should not know the sources of the information but should be permitted to provide a written answer if he desires. He should initial and date each report to indicate he has read it.

At the time of each annual evaluation, his rating should be reviewed with the executive. He should also initial and date the rating to indicate he has seen it.

All of the personnel file information will then be available for consideration in any promotion or required disciplinary action.

Executive Personnel Forms

General personnel forms were covered in the previous chapter. The two forms proposed here extend these to cover executives. These forms should also be on letter size sheets, printed on both sides if necessary.

The executive forms should not ask for information the company does not need. People naturally resent forms, and long, complicated ones encourage generalized answers. They are hard to fill out and hard to read when completed. The forms should be kept concise, readable and usable, limited to one sheet of paper if possible.

There should be one form for financial information and one for personal information. Verification and later comparison will be much easier if the two forms are separate pieces of paper. Periodic resubmission will also be easier to accomplish, since the times of resubmission will not be the same for both forms. Special problems in one area may require frequent resubmission of one form.

The forms will vary in content according to the needs of various kinds of businesses. The questions and instructions should be concise. Ample space should be allowed for complete handwritten answers. The forms should conclude with a signed statement that the information given is complete and correct.

Financial information is more easily read and understood in columnar form. The bank information section could have column headings across the page as follows:

Bank Name & Location   Type of Deposit   Present Balance

The instructions preceding these columns could state: "List all accounts of all kinds in banks and savings institutions including time deposits, certifications of deposit, savings accounts and checking accounts."

In the portion of the form listing debts of various types, it is important to include a column for interest rate paid and another for monthly payment amounts. It will be useful to have the monthly payment column on the far right. This will make it easy to compile the total of the monthly obligations for comparison with total monthly income. It will also stress to the executive filling out the form the importance of this information to management. It may then also become important to him to maintain these totals within manageable limits.

Columnar listing of some personal information will also make comparison easier. Personal information of this type includes dues and average monthly payments to clubs and social organizations, and average monthly cost of hobbies such as flying or golf. Columnar listing of names and locations can be made as in the financial information above.

Organization memberships should show the type of use made of them, for better understanding of their costs. For instance, (F) could indicate family use, (A) for adults only, (S) for self only, and (C) for children only. These memberships should be listed individually and the list should be complete. Changes in memberships or in amounts spent on each one can then be noted easily in later resubmissions of the form.

Financial Information

Each executive should make a full disclosure of his financial condition at the time he is hired. As noted above, this should be on a separate form that will contain only financial information. Its purpose is to show present net worth and present financial obligations.

The first information requested should be similar to that contained in current assets in a balance sheet: bank balances, savings deposits, stocks and bonds and all other liquid assets. It should include a listing of other sources of income such as inheritance or trust, wife's employment, rent income, and other business income. This will show family financial status, not just the status of the individual executive.

Other listings should include:

Fixed assets and obligations involved in their purchase:

- Home or other real estate — value, date of purchase, who holds mortgages, in what amounts, at what interest rate, current payment obligations.
- Interest in a business — kind, value, contingent liabilities.

Car

- When purchased
- Where financed
- Payment obligations
- Type and extent of insurance coverage.

Charge accounts and credit cards used regularly:

- What are the present unpaid amounts owed to each?
- Are time payments being made on appliances or related purchases?
- If so, what are present unpaid balances and amounts of required monthly payments?

Personal loans from banks or other loan agencies:

- Present balances
- Interest rates
- Monthly payments

These may seem to be stringent request for personal information, but experience proves why the employer should learn these details. The author once personally employed two men without getting financial information from them. They were talented in their field but neither had personal fiscal responsibility. One of them was so obligated at the time of hiring that his salary would barely cover the payments he had to make. The other became a compulsive buyer of personal gadgets whenever he and his wife had an argument over money. One of these men filed personal bankruptcy and the other ran away from his job and family financial problems. What is suggested here is based on personal experience as well as the experience of many companies. The company's financial responsibility requires that it establish the financial responsibility of its executives.

After an executive has furnished the financial information requested, the data should be reviewed with him to check its completeness. He may have forgotten to list the car used by his son or daughter in college. He may have omitted personal loans. The company should be sure to have complete information or be able to prove later that the executive failed to provide pertinent information requested. The form should end with his signature below a statement that sets out the penalty for willful failure to provide full information.

The items listed here are not all-inclusive. They are intended as a guide to show why financial information is important in hiring an executive. A personal interview should always follow to explore other possible obligations.

The information obtained on the financial form needs to be reviewed and tabulated thoroughly. Has the man shown that he can handle his own financial affairs? Can he pay what he owes without financial strain? Is he so obligated that the need to meet payments would make him easily tempted? The information on this form helps the employer rate the man's future relative honesty. It will show whether the company will make a wise investment in hiring or promoting him.

Personal Information

The personal information form will indicate how the executive and his family live, what their social aspirations are, and what forms of recreation they enjoy. Taken with the financial information, the personal data will indicate whether the family lives within its means. It will also show how closely knit the family is and consequently how stable it is. All of this bears on the executive's relative position as a security risk. It also indicates whether stresses at home may complicate his executive stresses. Changes in information on this form in succeeding submissions also show life style changes pertinent to the probability of his becoming a security risk.

This form should call for listing all organization memberships, including business, social and professional organizations in which membership requires payment of a fee or regular dues. These may sometimes be a combination of business and social activity. A business club that serves lunch and has a bar would be an example. This would require listing monthly social charges as well as membership fees. Are these purely personal memberships or are families also considered members? Is the executive now an officer of such a club?

If he belongs to a civic club, is he an officer or active in any other way aside from attendance? Does he take part in charity activities?

Information on professional organizations may indicate what his real business interests are. What professional studies has he undertaken with them?

An executive's social and recreational activities can indicate his attitude toward his work. If he enjoys his work there is a carry-over into his private life. He will associate with people in similar positions in other companies. He will associate with outsiders whom he meets in his work, and he will belong to clubs where these people are members. These will generally be activities that are within the financial range of his executive level. These social activities will increase his worth to the employer because he will draw on the experience of others as he associates with them.

In contrast, an executive with a different attitude toward his work will belong only to "status" clubs and organizations. He will be more interested in appearing with socially important people than with those on the same executive level. He will drive a larger car, have a longer boat and belong to more expensive clubs. All of these habits cost money. If he belongs to a country club, does he play much golf? If he belongs to a yacht club, does he do much sailing? Do his memberships include his family, or are they a substitute for family life?

The executive's outside interests should be evaluated for anything that will add to or conflict with his value as an executive. In every instance, the company should determine whether the executive's outside interests cost him more than he can afford to spend.

Periodic Resubmission of Information

Both financial and personal information forms should be required again before each promotion and at stated intervals where no promotion is involved.

Each promotion calls for a re-evaluation of the executive's financial and social position. Resubmission of these forms will permit comparison with prior forms. Is he more heavily in debt? What types of new debts are involved? If his debts have decreased, what type of debts is he paying off? Is he joining new social groups? Has he materially changed his life style?

These comparisons will indicate whether the executive is living within his means and whether he is properly planning his family's future. The company should look for changes which indicate any personal weaknesses. He may be spending too much on a home in a high status neighborhood. Is his status likely to require more money than he earns? Have his investments grown faster than his income accounts for?

None of these are solid evidence by themselves, but they indicate trends. Are they safe trends or crisis trends? The employer should project these trends a few years ahead to see if they show strength or weakness.

Each promotion moves an executive into more select company. Each step up condenses more responsibility into fewer jobs. Not all executives will be promoted, because there are always fewer jobs at the next higher level.

Some will stop at a particular level or job from choice. They like what they are doing, or they want no more responsibility, or they do not want to relocate to an area where promotion is available. Others do not progress because they lack the ability, education, training or personality required by the next step up. Regardless of the reason, the security risk does not stop with lack of promotion. Therefore the financial and personal information needs to be brought up-to-date periodically, at least every five years and sometimes as often as every three years. It should not be so often as to seem arbitrary, but it should be done when needed.

Honesty is a precious commodity. Executive financial and personal information reports help the company protect and encourage honesty.

CASE HISTORY #8

The president of Arctura Corporation is the company's principal stock-holder. He exercises control over corporate matters but is not very active in daily operations. His son has a close friend, Bob Richards, who is sales manager of a local automobile sales agency from which the president has bought personal cars. Based on the son's recommendation, and on his own knowledge of Richards' outgoing personality, the president hired Richards for an executive position in Arctura's purchasing department. Purchases of automotive equipment and supplies are under his jurisdiction.

Richards belongs to the local country club and regularly frequents a bar known to be a center for betting on sports events. He also plays poker regularly with a group that meets in a room above the bar. He owns a big car and a 25-foot cabin cruiser berthed at a nearby lake. His two children go to a private school. He is buying a large house in the country club subdivision.

He has paid only the interest on his house mortgage for the last three months. He owes two personal loan companies, and is regularly posted at the country club for late payment of monthly charges.

At the end of the first fiscal year after Richards was hired, the annual audit report shows a material increase in the unit cost of repairs, outside services, gasoline use and parts for all automotive equipment. An outside investigator, given access to Arctura records, determines that the company has been paying padded invoices for these charges. Padded charges of $20,000 are identified. The investigation further determines that Richards approved all the padded charges.

One tire supplier, when threatened with a civil recovery suit, admits that Richards set up a kickback scheme at the time he was hired by Arctura. The supplier had paid Richards $2,000 in kickback payments in eight months. Invoices are also found at the tire company showing that two Arctura purchasing employees working under Richards had purchased tires for their personal cars at very low prices.

Richards is discharged by Arctura. He has no assets from which any recovery can be made.

QUESTIONS

1. How were Bob Richards' debts pertinent to his qualifications as an executive?
2. What information should Arctura Corporation have obtained from Richards before hiring him as an executive?
3. How could the kickback schemes have been prevented?

Chapter 10

Honesty in Purchasing

Material diversion and kickback schemes are related purchasing problems. Only the degree of opportunity in a particular business operation determines which may be used or whether both may be used at once. Purchasing accountability cannot be effective unless two simple rules are followed:

1. All purchasing must be done through the purchasing department.
2. All purchased material must be verified as received.

Value Limitations of Raw Materials

Some raw materials are so low in value that they offer little theft temptation to employees. The cost of moving the material after stealing it may be more than its value as stolen property, or the places where it could be processed after theft may be too limited to present a profitable market. Various ores fit these conditions.

Each company presents an individual security problem in its procurement of raw materials and supplies. Availability, value, and market as stolen property should all be considered. Some companies own their own sources of raw materials. Petrochemical companies, for example, sometimes own their own oil and gas wells. Paper mills sometimes own the timberlands where they grow their own raw materials. Some fabricating businesses, on the other hand, use another company's finished product as a raw material. This more salable commodity is obviously more tempting to the thief.

All companies buy processing materials, supplies and equipment. These are often valuable enough to tempt employees. Their small volume and resulting smaller total value may limit their attractiveness to thieves. Again, availability, value and market should be guidelines in planning protection.

Lowering temptation levels, however, does not eliminate temptation. Sometimes it merely changes its direction.

Diversion Before Delivery

Actual theft of material after receipt is a recognized threat, one which most present-day security systems make some attempt to control. Temptation may change its direction, however, to diversion before delivery. Although diversion can cause large losses, the possibility is seldom considered by present-day security systems.

Diversion can take two forms. In the first form, a truck driver making deliveries to a plant retains part of the shipment. A lazy receiving clerk accepts the packing slip count instead of counting for himself. Knowing this, the truck driver makes the diversion for his own profit. Or the receiving clerk and the truck driver may work together and both profit from the diversion. Diversions of this type are usually limited in size but are very easy to accomplish. Income from them is not likely to be large, because large diversions would be noted soon by production shortages, and because the stolen materials suffer an immediate loss in value of 50% or more.

Non-Delivery and Over-Pricing

A much more lucrative form of diversionary theft is one that pays the supplier for over-priced material or for material never shipped. A scheme that pays the supplier for unshipped or over-priced material requires the cooperation of one or more employees of the purchaser. These may be employees in purchasing, receiving or accounting. Cooperation is obtained by paying the employee a portion of the extra profit the supplier receives from the plan. This payment is called a kickback.

Kickback schemes can be started by the supplier or by the purchaser's employees. The puchaser's employee can be anyone in a position to change a receiving record or approve an invoice for payment. At the supplier's end a kickback plan usually requires participation of a top executive. The extra payment the supplier receives is part of a check from the purchaser, payable to the supplier company. It must, therefore, go through the supplier's bank account. A kickback is paid in cash or in items bought with cash. Drawing the money from the supplier's bank account requires the signature of a company executive.

Preventing all types of diversion is the aim of accountability in the purchasing and receiving departments. Examples of how this can be done are given in this chapter and the following chapter on receiving.

Splitting Commissions

A different form of kickback, one that seems less serious on the surface, is commission splitting. The salesman pays part of his sales commission to the purchasing agent. At the start of such a payment plan, the purchasing company often suffers no loss. The purchased product is needed and its quality is as good as the competing product previously purchased.

The salesman merely promises part of his sales commission to the purchasing agent. All the purchasing agent has to do is change suppliers. No one suffers yet. The salesman makes part of a commission he previously did not make at all. The buyer pockets extra cash each time the salesman is paid his commission. Both now profit where neither profited previously.

This scheme nevertheless is a dangerous one; most kickbacks seem to carry a contagion. A purchasing agent who accepts a commission split soon finds other kickback schemes to add to his income. Greed takes over. The extra income soon looms larger than his responsibilities to his employer.

Security should question any sudden, unexplained change in source of major purchased items. Production departments, stockrooms and accounts payable employees can provide such information to security.

Losses from various kickback schemes can easily cost a company more than physical theft or diversion. Kickbacks are easy to start. Once started they often continue for years, until discovered by accident . . . or by accountability procedures.

Gifts from Suppliers

Buyers should not accept gifts of any size from suppliers or salesmen. Such a gift is really a bribe or a rebate that belongs to the buyer's employer. If a buyer feels he is entitled to such a gift, it is because he has favored the person or company offering it.

Lunch meetings between salesmen and buyers often permit legitimate uninterrupted exchange of useful information. These lunches should be paid for on a reciprocal basis with no favors asked or given. This can best be controlled by a budget set up in the purchasing department for this purpose. Buyers can reclaim lunch expenses by a petty cash slip filled out after each lunch they pay for, or charge accounts may be set up at restaurants patronized by the buyers.

The purchasing agent should control lunch expenditures to be sure that all buyers make them. A buyer who seldom draws on these funds may have poor personal relations with salesmen, or he may be allowing the salesmen to pay for all lunches. Either instance calls for supervisory action.

Large Volume Purchases

As mentioned previously, some raw materials are too low in value to be profitable to the thief. This does not mean, however, that they should be omitted from all security consideration. Raw materials may not be subject to physical theft, but failure-to-deliver thefts are most profitable where they involve large volume, routinely purchased materials. Daily deliveries of bulk raw materials can easily be over-measured regularly.

Example: Ten truckloads of a raw material are received daily at a plant. The same trucks are used every day. The bare weight (tare) of each truck is established the first time it is used. The scale house has a list of these weights. Each truck is weighed in full each time it makes a delivery. The empty truck is not weighed as it leaves. The scale man simply deducts the previously established tare from the full weight recorded. He reports the difference as the weight of the raw material received.

Suppose that, after the bare weight of a truck is established at the scale house, a 100-pound lead weight is placed under the driver's seat. Every truckload delivered is recorded by the scale house as 100 pounds heavier than actual delivery. The supplier is paid for 100 pounds more per truckload than he delivered.

This sort of diversion does not require cooperation from the purchaser's employees or from the truck drivers, although it may involve either or both. Lack of accountability is all that is really required.

Protection against this form of diversion requires only the second, verifying count that is the essence of accountability. This is obtained by picking two or three trucks at random to go back on the scales each day, empty. Any truck that is overweight when empty should be held isolated until security can check it over. If diversion is established, the security investigation must consider the possibility of employee participation. A kickback scheme affords the supplier a measure of protection. He has a friend in the opposite camp. The kickback payment is a bribe to secure this protection.

Thus, even low value raw materials require some protection by accountability procedures.

Special Materials

Many kickback schemes start with some processing department convincing management that their supplies are too special for regular purchasing — that only people in their own department are competent to purchase them. They are therefore given purchase order forms and complete control over quantities, quality and price. They may even try to control their own receiving. If they approve invoices for payment, all control is lost. Purchasing accountability requires centralized purchasing procedures regardless of the specialized nature of the materials used. Any technical assistance needed should be supplied through the purchasing department.

Accountability can usually be obtained by two independent counts or tallies taken at or near the same location. Security then needs only to compare these counts.

Purchasing accountability must include the supplier's invoice. Security does not have access to the supplier's shipping tally. Quantities and prices on the invoice therefore must be verified by accountability procedures after both materials and invoice are received.

Forms Distribution for Accountability

Purchasing accountability requires an entirely independent and accurate count of what is received. Copies of this independent tally must go to three separate departments: purchasing, accounts payable, and material stockroom. There they meet other records to provide the comparisons required by security. The following plan of forms preparation and distribution illustrates how this can be accomplished.

Purchase orders are usually prepared from a requisition of some kind, giving quantity and quality, along with other details necessary to ensure correct purchasing. The purchasing department then adds unit price. The purchase order, when prepared, then contains the three items required for accountability:

1. Quantity
2. Description (type and quality)
3. Unit price.

The purchase order is one of those prenumbered forms mentioned in Chapter 7, with one copy filed numerically where it is prepared. The purchasing employee who compiles the information for the purchase order should sign at least the file copy, establishing responsibility for the information on the form.

There should be sufficient copies of the purchase order form so that one goes to each of the following for accountability purposes:

1. Purchasing Department working copy
2. Purchasing Department numerical file
3. Accounts Payable Department
4. Receiving Department.

(See Figure 2, Purchase Order Form Flow Chart.)

These will be identical copies except that the receiving copy must *not* show the quantities ordered. The receiving clerk cannot make an independent count if he knows the quantities he should be receiving. This presents no technical problem for the supplier of the blank form: the receiving copy can be prepared so there is no carbon paper where the quantities are shown, or this part of the form can be perforated and torn off before the form goes to the receiving department.

The receiving clerk will have all the other information he needs to complete his separate receiving tally form. He must make his own count.

For business use this receiving tally form is prepared as a routine function of the receiving department. For purchasing accountability this form is vital to security. It is even more important that it be prepared correctly.

The separate tally, or receiving report, is another form that requires prenumbering. Three copies will be required for purchase accountability. Another copy is filed numerically where prepared.

One of these three accountability tally form copies goes directly to the accounting section that records and pays accounts payable. The proper accountability use of this tally form requires

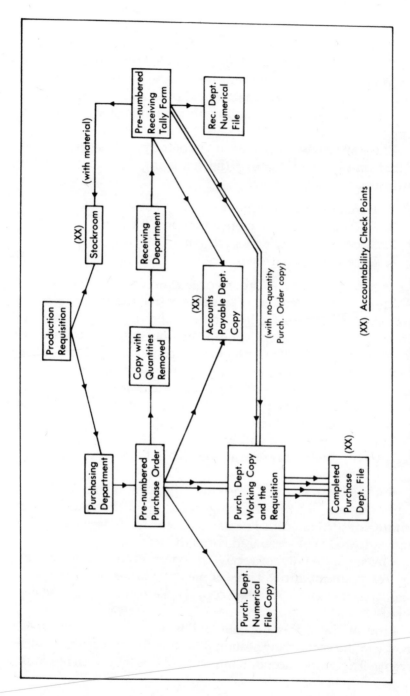

Figure 2. Purchase Order Form Flow Chart

that all suppliers' invoices also go directly to the accounts payable section. There the invoice will be checked against the purchase order for price and quantity, and against the receiving tally for quantity and quality. If the invoice meets these three accountability checkpoints, it can be paid without further authorization.

The receiving tally form, the purchase order, the supplier's invoice, and the numbered voucher or check copy make up a completed package which the accounts payable department files in an inactive file.

A second copy of the tally form goes with the received material to the point where it is stored or used. A copy of the requisition is also sent there. This copy will be discussed in greater detail in the next chapter.

A third copy of the receiving tally will be attached to receiving's copy of the purchase order. These will be sent to the purchasing department.

If the receiving tally shows that less than the ordered quantity was received, purchasing must determine the reason. If no more is to be shipped, this should be documented before the purchasing department files its completed order package. This documentation should go with the order packages into the inactive file.

Back Orders

If the received quantity is less than ordered, and further shipments are to be made, a back order should be prepared. The back order form should also be prenumbered. It should be given the same distribution as the original order except that no copy need go to the supplier.

Each succeeding back order will show the original purchase order number and any preceding back order number. This will provide continuity from the original through the receipt of material on the final back order.

Each time purchasing prepares a back order, the preceding uncompleted purchase order or back order package will go to inactive files. If a new back order must be made for unshipped balances, that new back order should be the only active record, so that purchasing has a record only of what remains to be shipped.

Back orders will have the same internal distribution as a new order. These should be the only information given to accounts payable and receiving of what is to be received and paid for. In particular, the receiving department should not have retained anything about the original order. For accountability purposes the receiving department should only receive, count, and report what it counts.

Confusion in the purchasing department is greatly reduced by issuing a new back order after each uncompleted shipment. Marking the original order with what is or is not shipped through several partial shipments can easily cause loss of control. Accountability records in purchasing and accounts payable would soon show disagreement. In order to maintain security, extra record checking would be required, at extra expense. If this loss of control happens often, it will soon be accepted as normal. When confusion becomes normal, security is lost.

The company must try to operate an accountability system that prevents such breakdown in control. It must also be alert for intended breakdown of security measures caused by those employees who cannot steal when the system works. Employees who seem to have trouble understanding a security system may actually know the system well enough to make it break down.

The supplier does not need to receive copies of the back order forms prepared by the purchasing department. These back orders are tools of the purchaser's internal accountability system. The supplier will have his own internal system for recording what is unshipped.

Security Checks

Security will check the numerical sequence of all prenumbered forms in the numerical files in each department. Any gaps or misuse should be investigated.

Security will compare the completed order files in purchasing and accounts payable. The frequency of these comparisons will vary depending on security requirements. Any changes or differences on forms attached to the same order in purchasing or accounts payable should be investigated. In particular, changes in price or quantity in one file should be verified in the other file. All changes should be authenticated in both files.

If one receiving tally shows a changed quantity, all other copies of the same tally number should show the same change. The receiving tally is the principal purchasing accountability form. It can only be effective as an accountability record if its accuracy is checked constantly. It is part of the permanent record in purchasing, accounts payable, and material stockroom. Another copy is in the numerical file in the receiving department. Each of these places uses it independently of the others. A kickback scheme involving short delivery could operate only if this form is changed in one or more of these places. Security checking of these forms against each other will prevent or disclose kickback schemes.

Each employee who prepares one of these prenumbered forms for accountability use must sign the form he prepares. It may also be useful to have employees who process these forms initial them as processed. Responsibility for any deviation in use can then be localized. If additional accountability is needed, someone in the accounting department, not connected with paying accounts payable, can audit the accounts payable finished purchase order packages before they are filed in the inactive file. This audit is already used by some companies to check price extensions and to catch errors in payment of supplier invoices. Only a small extra step would verify that all necessary forms are present and agree with each other.

Once an accountability system is established, the forms used in it should be checked regularly to ensure compliance. Any deviation from established rules should be investigated. The employee responsible should be identified. Even when they are not theft-connected, these errors must be brought to the attention of the responsible employee and his supervisor.

Developing Employee Responsibility

No accountability system can succeed unless it builds into itself a system of responsibility for error and omission. If this conditioning influence is missing, accountability will erode. Employees must know what the accountability procedures are and feel responsible for their part in them.

Testing Your Own System

It might be a good exercise at this point for the reader to review his own system of purchasing. Imagine that you are a dishonest employee looking for weaknesses you can exploit for your personal profit. Until you recognize the weaknesses in your own system, you cannot properly apply accountability measures in your business. Security measures should be applied only where they will reduce temptation and theft. Applying them where employees know they are not needed will only demonstrate a management weakness.

Example: A Kickback Scheme

The following is for those who read the suggestion in the preceding paragraph and did nothing.

In a city of over 100,000 population, the governing body was an elected commission. Each commissioner was responsible for specific service departments in the city government.

One of the city commissioners had been in office for about 30 years. His re-election had become routine, both to him and the voters. There had been rumors that he and some of his supervisors were living much more comfortably than their salaries would have permitted. Several years earlier, one supervisor had been convicted of pocketing money taken in by city parking lots. This supervisor served his sentence without revealing what he had done with the money.

Each commissioner was master over purchasing in his department. When he approved an invoice, it was paid without question by the city finance department.

A complex investigation of purchases in this commissioner's office resulted in his indictment and the indictments of two of his supervisors for assorted thefts from the city. The commissioner was tried and convicted of theft of city funds totaling over $80,000 during a period of two-and-a-half years. This included only those amounts that could be supported by strong substantial evidence.

Most of these thefts came from payments by the city for undelivered truck tires. Most of these tires were recorded as purchased from regular tire sources who were willing to bill for undelivered tires. There was one fictitious company set up to help in the scheme. It even had business stationery and a bank account. Another semi-legitimate company involved was run by a close relative of a supervisor.

Because tires were purchased legitimately from some of these sources, it was often impossible to identify fictitious invoices. Testimony of others involved in the scheme was used extensively in the trial. This testimony also proved the payment of kickback money to supervisors, and through them to the commissioner.

The city had no purchasing rules or procedures to prove delivery of anything. Purchase order numbers were sometimes used to authorize purchases from a supplier with the purchase order later made from the suppliers' invoices. The city paid whatever the commissioner approved.

There was also testimony about other items paid for by the city but never delivered. One supplier said the commissioner and one of his supervisors called on him about a new kitchen for the commissioner's home. The city officials openly asked him to supply what was needed and to bill it to the city as copper pipe and fittings. The supplier did so to protect his legitimate business with the city. The city paid for the commissioner's new kitchen.

Very few city officials work under an accountability system that would prevent kickback schemes. The guilty commissioner in this case and the employees under him had no trouble finding some suppliers willing to make a dishonest dollar. Most suppliers in private business are no different. Everything the commissioner did could be done by most branch managers in business . . . if there is no accountability system. All that is required for a kickback scheme are two dishonest people and a weak security system.

CASE HISTORY #9

At Arctura, the purchasing department types a purchase order number on each purchase order as it is prepared. The buyer mails the original to a supplier. He retains all other copies. The receiving department is supposed to call for a copy when any material is received.

All purchase invoices come to the purchasing department for matchup with the purchase order. The invoice is then approved by the buyer and sent to accounts payable as approved for payment.

One copy of the completed purchase order then goes with the material to the storeroom or plant area where the requisition originated. Another copy is supposed to be filed in the purchasing department in an alphabetical file under the name of the supplier.

An Arctura Corporation buyer arranged with a supplier to have the supplier submit invoices covering issued purchase orders without shipping the material. The buyer then approved the invoices for payment and destroyed all copies of the purchase orders. The buyer received a kickback payment from the supplier in the form of monthly payments on a car purchased by the buyer.

QUESTIONS

1. How could evidence of the kickback scheme described above have been detected?
2. What primary change should be made in the purchase order form?
3. What distribution of the purchase order copies is required by accountability?
4. Which one of these distributed copies is the key one for accountability?

Chapter 11

Plugging Leaks in Receiving

The receiving department is an intermediate step between requisition and use of materials. Its function is mechanical; it records receipt of material. It has no direct effect on what is produced or how it is produced. Its importance to accountability in other departments is therefore not always recognized. Nevertheless, receiving is a vital link in preventing kickback schemes in purchasing, accounts payable and inventories. An accountability system therefore overlaps in these departments, and part of what is recommended here is also covered in the preceding chapter on purchasing.

The Receiving Tally

The receiving form or tally is the foundation on which purchasing accountability is built, and it should be prepared precisely and accurately. It should be a prenumbered form in at least four copies. The same four copies will also serve most of the non-security functions required of the form. Their use for accountability thus adds no cost.

The receiving form should be devised so it can be filled in by hand by the clerk as he counts. He should sign it and add whatever information is needed to identify it with the purchase order copy previously sent to him.

In one sample system, the receiving department receives four copies of the purchase order containing all information except the quantities ordered. The receiving clerk records the quantities as he counts them and signs his count. He dates the receipt and distributes the copies. This procedure saves receiving time because only the quantities and date received must be written in by the clerk. The balance of the receiving tally information is included when the purchase order is typed. This system does away with the prenumbered tally form, so one copy remains with the receiving department, filed numerically by purchase order number. Thus the receiving clerk always has all purchase order numbers accounted for either in his received file or in his file of unreceived purchase orders.

Distribution of Tallies

The copies of the tally required for accountability will be distributed as follows:

1. Accounts Payable Department
2. Purchasing Department
3. Stockroom (with the received material)
4. Receiving Department numerical file.

Figure 2 in the preceding chapter shows the flow of these receiving tally forms.

The accounts payable copy shows the quantity for which payment is then authorized. It also shows quality and similar information for comparison with the same data on the purchase order. *Since this is the only place where the supplier's invoice enters accountability, all invoice variables must be checked here for accuracy.* These should include all factors that could allow payment for quantity, quality or price differing from what was ordered or received.

The purchasing department copy is attached to the receiving department copy of the purchase order. Both then go to the purchasing department to show if the order is completed or if a back order is needed. The purchasing department controls the quantities to be received. It needs the receiving tally for this purpose. Purchasing can also help make sure that the stated quality received matches that required by the requisition and purchase order. While purchasing does not inspect the received material, it can detect descriptions or stock numbers that differ materially from what was ordered.

The next copy goes with the material to a stockroom or some other location where the material will be available for production. This location will also have received a copy of the requisition. The source of the requisition and the place where the material is to be stored can both be shown on the requisition and the purchase order. This information is usually part of the accounting system that allocates costs to different departments.

The storeroom that receives the material from the receiving department should immediately verify quantity and quality as received with the receiving tally and the requisition. Any differences should be reported first to security. If the tally matches the material received, that fact should be noted on the tally. The tally should then be signed by the verifier and attached to the file copy of the requisition.

This completes the full circle from preparation of the requisition to receipt of the material at the point of origin of the requisition.

There are three places in the receiving cycle where the tally is compared with other forms: the requisition, purchase order, and supplier's invoice. These forms are prepared in places with different responsibilities and each place uses the tally for a different purpose. Accountability can be obtained if these three places simply perform their normal business functions accurately. Security merely ensures performance by comparing different copies of the same forms.

The Packing Slip

A packing slip usually comes with the material received. In some instances it is a copy of the delivery ticket which the receiving clerk signs for the delivery truck driver. The receiving clerk needs this packing slip to verify that delivery has been made of the quantities he signs for. He should not accept the count on the packing slip without making a verifying count for himself.

Giving the receiving clerk access to the packing slip is a threat to accountability almost equal to giving him the quantities on the purchase order. It is relatively easy to make sure he does not know the quantities on the purchase orders, but little can be done to deny him access to the quantities on packing slips. This is a point of weakness that requires added security measures.

The packing slip should be attached to the numerical file copy of the corresponding receiving slip. These are filed in the receiving department.

If there is no accountability system, a receiving clerk can become part of a kickback scheme with suppliers with little fear of exposure. All he needs to do is make a receiving slip agreeing with a packing slip that lists more than was actually received. The supplier makes out his invoice for the inflated quantity shown on the packing slip. The supplier gets paid for more than he ships. He kicks back part of his illegal profit to the receiving clerk.

In a proper accountability system the copy of the receiving slip going with the material would have to show actual receipts. In this event, comparison of all copies of the receiving tally by security would show any disagreement. The inflated quantity would be corrected to the actual quantity received by the storeroom.

Since requisitions will originate in many different departments, the receiving clerk could not arrange collusion in all of them. Security can make its own verifying counts of material received, on a spot basis, in most departments. The mere presence of security in this activity will deter temptation to collusion.

Security should provide greater protection where greater temptation is present. Experience shows that large regular purchases offer greater kickback potential than irregular, higher value, large purchases. Regular purchases from one supplier become very routine all along the line; what is done from habit requires little attention. Without conscious thought no count will be accurate.

If the receiving clerk is honest but lazy, he will copy information from the packing slip instead of making his own count. Security should check the wording on the numerical file copies of tallies with the wording on attached packing slips. The lazy clerk will use terminology from the packing slip instead of from the purchase order copy. He will copy misspellings and show wrong amounts received. If he copies rather than counts, a good security system will soon find out.

Numerical Copy File

The tally copies filed numerically in the receiving department will have packing slips attached to them. These forms must be available to security until the last back order is shipped on each original order. The prenumbered receiving tally form is the foundation of purchasing and receiving accountability, and it should be treated accordingly. This includes keeping it available until all possible use has been made of it in every department.

Shortcomings in Receiving

There will usually be less space assigned to the receiving department than to shipping. Since materials are usually purchased in quantities larger than average sale quantities, the number of individual purchases is smaller than the number of sales shipments. The receiving clerk does not need to bother with routing or shipping methods. In short, receiving is considered less important than shipping. Security seldom pays any attention to receiving.

In one plant, the receiving clerk only worked at receiving as a secondary job. Deliveries were unloaded in an open, unattended area. The receiving clerk signed delivery slips without verifying them. He then made out receiving slips later in the day when his other duties slackened off. He had no knowledge of what had actually been received. He never knew if a shortage was caused by short delivery or by theft from the receiving area.

Some special processing materials may even be received directly in the department where they are to be used. In one instance a painting department was allowed to order and receive the paint it used. The high prices paid for common paints and thinners alerted an investigator to a kickback scheme.

In another plant, materials were delivered to two separate areas convenient to their points of use. One receiving clerk could not be in both places at once. A plant foreman was signing the receiving clerk's name to receiving slips in one of the locations. When a shipment was counted short in the stockroom there was no way to prove responsibility.

Receiving crews can be assigned other duties if receiving activity does not keep them busy. In one plant, for example, receiving clerks were assigned housekeeping duties in nearby manufacturing areas. In another company, two order-filling lift truck operators were trained as receiving clerks. The gate guards used a public address system to alert them when a shipment came in.

Regardless of what other work they do, receiving clerks must be trained in receiving procedures before they can be held responsible for security violations. They must know their responsibilities and be capable of assuming them. In addition, untrained people make more errors, and correcting these errors often costs more than preventing them.

Isolate the Receiving Department

For security reasons, receiving should be physically separated from shipping. Fences should be used if there is no other way of separating the departments.

Dock areas usually contain vending machines and rest rooms. Employees and outside truck drivers move about freely. It is hard enough to isolate truck drivers from material on the dock if shipping and receiving are separated; exposure is multiplied when employees and drivers from both departments are mingled. Higher temptation will cause more thefts. Isolation is the first step toward security.

If the receiving department is large enough to have full-time employees, they should be paid a salary instead of hourly wages. Receiving is not part of production; it is more closely related to the accounting department. Its employees should be salaried to further this identification with administrative functions. Its supervision should come from accounting or some other administrative section outside of purchasing.

The most practical method of isolating receiving is to put it in a separate building where only receiving employees are admitted. Received material can be checked in and placed in bays representing the requisitioning areas or functions. When the requisitioners come to pick up their material, it will be delivered through an exit from the receiving department by a receiving employee. This sort of system will provide the easiest flow of material, the best security against theft, and the lowest security cost.

Bulk Deliveries

There are some materials that cannot be brought into a receiving area because of their nature or method of delivery. These require special receiving methods and special security precautions.

In one plant, for example, a resinous liquid was received by tank car and dumped directly into a storage tank. All that was required for security purposes and receiving records was that a clerk, without knowledge of the capacity of the tank car, measure the storage tanks before and after the car dumped its load. The difference was the quantity to be shown as received.

Most bulk materials like this are low enough in value to make outright theft improbable. The previously discussed distribution of receiving tally copies for accountability purposes provides the necessary protection against kickback schemes. Security problems change, however, with a product of higher cash value.

Example: Gasoline for automotive use within a plant was brought in by tank truck. It was dumped from the truck into a conveniently accessible storage tank. A receiving clerk read the meter on the truck after it dumped its load and recorded his reading on the receiving tally. The delivery ticket the truck driver gave him contained the meter reading of the truck when it left the bulk oil plant. The difference between these two figures was the amount shown as received. No record was made of amounts pumped out of the storage tank for in-plant use, since there was little chance for employees to divert any to personal use. The only record of amount used was the receiving tally.

As a routine part of a security survey, the storage tank was measured before and after the truck made a delivery. The receiving slip showed about 50 gallons more received than actual measurement recorded. The truck had not delivered all the meter said it did.

Surveillance was conducted of the truck on its next delivery to the plant. En route from the bulk oil plant to the customer's plant, the truck driver detoured into an independent filling station. He drove behind the station where he could not be seen from the street and filled several cans from the truck. He then drove to the plant to make his scheduled delivery, unloading about 50 gallons less than the receiving clerk recorded from the truck gauge.

Further observation showed the same driver making about one trip daily behind the independent filling station. His route included various industrial plants where he delivered gasoline in bulk quantities. He was giving this independent station a portion of gas at the expense of his employer's customers, and he was adding about $7.00 per day to his salary in the process.

No employee of the customer plant could be shown to be in collusion with the driver. The small amounts diverted by the driver indicated this was his own private scheme. The plan was, however, capable of enough expansion to have included a receiving clerk.

The value of the product being delivered (gasoline) and its easy conversion into money made this a vulnerable operation.

Measuring the storage tank before and after the truck made a delivery provided one part of a new accountability system. Having the gate guard record the meter reading on the truck as it entered and departed from the plant provided the required second count. Comparison of these independent counts eliminated the danger point.

Any decision to receive material outside the regular receiving area should be cleared with security. A proper system of accountability can then be set up before temptation creates a problem.

CASE HISTORY #10

In the scheme outlined in Case History #7, the buyer was noted to be the person receiving the kickback payments. When the dishonesty was first suspected the only known factor was that there were no purchase order copies for the material that had been paid for.

At this point the investigators could assume one of four possibilities: (1) The material was received and then diverted by the receiving clerk. (2) The material was never shipped; the receiving clerk and the supplier were involved in a kickback scheme. (3) The material was never shipped; the buyer and the supplier were involved in a kickback scheme. (4) The material was received and diverted by the shipping clerk, with that clerk and the buyer having sold the material and divided the proceeds.

The missing material consisted of general plant maintenance and hardware items that did not go into production. Some were stock items and others were purchased only when needed.

The buyer blamed the shortages on the receiving clerk, and the receiving clerk blamed them on the buyer. Because of the lack of adequate records, an extensive and costly investigation had to be conducted before the buyer was established as the guilty party.

QUESTIONS

1. For accountability purposes, what distribution should be made of the receiving tally forms?
2. How would accountability use of the receiving tally prevent the kickback scheme from succeeding?

Chapter 12

Securing Inventories

Accountability is relatively easy to attain in the inventory portion of the production process. Motion of materials is more controlled here, and records of material flow already exist for production purposes. Purchasing, production and sales records are kept to ensure an even flow of finished products to meet sales demand. These inventory records provide most of what security needs in order to establish accountability in warehouse and storage areas.

Requisitions for Material Purchases

Some sort of requisition system is needed to keep production flowing smoothly. Orders of bulky raw materials must be scheduled in advance to meet projected production schedules. Purchasing may place a large bulk order with delivery schedules set each month, or a purchase order of a certain size may be issued each time the stockpile reaches a minimum level. Any bulk purchasing system depends on some storage level point to trigger a requisition for purchase of material.

Components, parts and non-bulk raw materials are more often kept in storerooms and warehouses and are withdrawn in day-to-day amounts to meet production schedules. In this case production makes a daily requisition; purchasing is triggered when stock reaches a pre-set low amount. There is a maximum and a minimum limit for each item. When the minimum quantity is reached, the storeroom prepares a purchase requisition for the quantity needed to re-establish the maximum. Under an accountability system, these requisitions become the first step in issuance of a purchase order.

When a storeroom receives a request for material from production, and that request triggers the necessity to re-order that material, this storeroom issues a requisition to the purchasing department. This requisition need not be a prenumbered form. The issuing storeroom keeps one copy for its own record. This is the first step in accountability as set out in the chapter on Purchasing and in the flow chart that is Figure 2. The storeroom is one of the accountability checkpoints on that chart.

Receiving Department Records

Each purchase order should show who is to get the ordered material when it is received. The material goes to the proper storage area, accompanied by a copy of the receiving tally. There should be verification at the storage point that the received material matches information on the requisition and the receiving tally as to quantity and quality. Any deviation should be reported directly to security for action. This is half of the minimum procedure required for purchasing and receiving accountability. This is the point where warehousing and storage accountability begins. Purchasing and receiving accountability guarantees the accuracy of accountability in warehousing and storage.

The rest of this chapter is concerned with the problems of accounting for this material through manufacture, sales and shipping operations.

Material Inventories

A purchased material comes under some sort of inventory control when it reaches a stockpile, storeroom or warehouse.

Methods and exactness of these inventory records will depend on the bulk, quantity, use in production, and value of the materials involved. Storerooms may vary from several acres of logs in an open stockpile to gold and silver ingots for metal contact use that are stored in a bank-type vault.

All types of inventory records will be subject to one control that is not primarily a part of security: production requirements. Production schedules for any manufactured or assembled product call for one or more of each part making up the finished product. Purchasing of each part is governed by the total number required to meet production schedules. If production of 1,000 units of Product A is scheduled each month, and each Product A requires 5 units of Part X in its production, then 5,000 units of Part X are required each month. Inventory records should be checked in the storeroom where Part X is stored. If inventory shows that 100 more units were requisitioned by production each month than could have been used, there is a security problem. Here is where an inventory kept for purchasing use becomes part of accountability.

Most production can be broken down into component parts or quantities of raw materials needed for completion. Comparing the quantities required with the withdrawals from inventories *at fairly regular intervals* will soon reveal any differences that may be signs of theft or diversion. This should be a security comparison made by the security department. The company should not depend on reports from production or storeroom personnel, who are production-oriented and cannot be expected to note all matters that indicate security problems. They may also be involved in thefts and diversions themselves.

Here again, security makes use of inventory records already kept for production and purchasing purposes. Nothing is added to costs except the security department payroll.

Production Flow Records

A continuous production line is usually fed by component production lines. Each of these sub-lines starts with raw material or parts taken from a storeroom. Inventory control for the sub-line follows the same pattern as for the main production line. The number of parts used to make the sub-production line's end product is determined; these totals are compared with the totals requisitioned from the storeroom for the sub-line. If more was requisitioned than was needed to complete the number of finished parts, there has been diversion.

This verification need not be accomplished on each sub-part going into the finished product. The value and availability for theft of various components will determine where security sets up its checkpoints. There will be many places along a production line where checks can be made. In some cases there may be one place where many sub-assemblies are combined, affording an excellent opportunity for one daily count to verify all parts used.

The process outlined above will not fit exactly into all types of businesses, but the basic system can be applied to various types of storeroom records. Accountability procedures must be applied somewhere between the start and finish of production to help localize losses.

In any production line, a certain amount of loss will be caused by faulty or broken parts or damage during production. These losses can be averaged out over a period of time to be figured into storeroom withdrawals as a constant factor. For example, a use figure might be established of 12.3 per unit where 12 represents actual production and .3 represents non-production loss. Security needs to check these figures to be sure such losses can be verified and that damaged or broken parts are kept for salvage value. Establishing these loss figures is important to production: a part with a high legitimate use loss needs to be redesigned or replaced.

Finished Inventory

The company's interest in finished inventory is twofold. The final number of finished products going into the storeroom provides a last checkpoint to determine if all purchased material went into the production of finished products. It makes possible a final determination of how many of each component were used in the finished products going into inventory.

Secondly, the company determines how many finished products are available for sale. Production schedules are tuned to this figure. Verification at this point by security is necessary to see if there was any diversion between the end of production and the warehousing of the finished product.

Every business has a finished product inventory which is used for many purposes. Security can use the same record for many security reasons without adding to its cost. Chapters 14 and 15 illustrate how this inventory is used for accountability purposes in the areas of sales records and shipping.

Finished inventory is a mid-point in accountability. It provides another checkpoint to determine whether employee dishonesty caused any losses of finished product or of cash in handling sales orders, shipping and accounting.

The finished product inventory itself is rather easily verified on paper. Production puts in so many items; sales takes out so many. The items present are compared with what should be present. This is a normal business procedure.

Security requires verification of these paper figures. Verification of what goes into the finished inventory, as we have seen, can be carried back to the requisitions for raw materials. Verification of withdrawals from finished inventory, as we shall learn in subsequent chapters, requires verification of sales orders, shipping orders, billing and payment for merchandise sales.

Preventing Large Storeroom Thefts

Chapter 5 described how physical security can prevent small, lunch-box-size thefts of goods for personal use. Here we are concerned with diversion or theft of goods from storerooms in commercial quantities. Theft of this size usually requires collusion by two or more people. Someone steals and a second person is needed to get the large quantity of stolen property out of the plant.

Accountability will not detect commercial quantity thefts immediately as they happen. Physical security measures may assist in catching the thief. Usually, however, the special efforts needed to catch a thief in the act are not started until after accountability has shown substantial losses. The expense of these efforts can become considerable. Physical security measures and their expense should be determined by the degree of honesty that can be maintained through an accountability system.

If storeroom materials are disappearing in commercial quantities, there are a few basic physical security measures that should be considered. Any large theft requires some means of transportation. The company should determine the physical size of its loss. How many cubic feet would the missing material occupy? Could it be put in small boxes? How much space would its length require? Does it need to be protected from weather? Answers to these and similar questions will reveal a great deal about how the property left the plant.

The storeroom's location in relation to receiving and shipping should be considered. The weight of the individual or packaged articles stolen will indicate whether they were carried or wheeled out of the storeroom. If forklift trucks that deliver material to the storeroom return to an area where there are trucks that come and go through plant gates, they may be used to deliver stolen goods to outgoing trucks.

Temptation in this area can be reduced by the installation of closed circuit television cameras for the obvious purpose of watching employees. Monitoring of these cameras can be on a random basis until a loss is recorded by these or other means. This area also lends itself to use of undercover employees after a loss is established.

The company should try to solve its loss problem within its plant area where it controls the protective measures. Law enforcement officials can then be used for surveillance and arrest of any outsiders involved in the theft itself and in the buying or selling of stolen material.

Firm evidence of storeroom losses calls for some corrective measures of a static nature. A Dutch door with a counter top may be needed to limit access to the storeroom. Access doors may need to be small enough so that lift trucks must drop and pick up their loads outside the storeroom. These static measures are easy to establish once a loss problem has been identified.

Waste and Trash

Although ordinary trash collection and disposal is a separate housekeeping problem, security must be concerned with the loss potential in this area. Any material valuable enough to require protection can produce waste that is of value. Waste material that is worth stealing should be given the protection its value warrants.

Residue of a bronze machining operation, for example, is even more valuable than a bronze casting. Both would be sold as scrap if stolen. Five pounds of residue would not take up as much space as five pounds of casting, nor would its removal be as likely to be noticed. Waste is always stolen for its resale value rather than for use. The thief who steals waste material will not make as much money as a buyer who takes a kickback, but the difference is only one of degree. The buyer merely has greater opportunity to profit from dishonesty. Both steal for profit.

The finished metal casting, plus the waste, should nearly equal the weight of the rough casting. The average percentage of material lost as scrap can be established; thereafter, security merely checks scrap weight against total use to be sure the waste percentage does not vary significantly.

Valuable material may be mixed with regular trash to be reclaimed after it is removed from the plant. This type of theft may be on a small scale but is usually for financial gain. Special accumulation points should be established for valuable trash, and security should find ways to be sure that valuable waste is accounted for at these points. Someone in the manufacturing process should be responsible for weighing waste material and taking it to its accumulation point.

Empty cartons should be compressed and bound so they do not become receptacles for stolen waste. Periodically, trash bins should be inspected while they are being emptied to be sure they contain nothing of value.

CASE HISTORY #11

The Arctura Corporation makes six different electronic products. Each uses an electronic switching relay of identical size and design. Some use only one relay while others use more than one. Other manufacturers use the same relay. Arctura stores the relays in one locked storeroom because they are small and cost about $3.00 each. They are re-ordered from the manufacturer when the storeroom inventory reaches a set minimum.

A security survey of Arctura operations totaled the production runs for a six-month period of each item using this relay and multiplied the total of each different item by the number of such relays used in it. This produced a total number of needed relays that was twenty percent less than the number actually taken out of the storeroom for that production period.

The survey made three general recommendations as a result of these findings:

• Determine which production line or lines had drawn more relays than were needed for production.
• Determine if this over-use was due to theft or faulty production methods.
• Set up an accountability system to disclose such losses in the future.

QUESTIONS

1. How could Arctura determine which production lines were drawing more relays than normal production required?
2. How could Arctura determine if the over-use was caused by theft or faulty production methods?
3. What specific accountability procedures are required to cure this problem of over-use, regardless of its cause?

Chapter 13

Controlling Production Thefts

Accountability is seldom accomplished completely in one limited area such as production, purchasing or shipping. Security is strengthened by comparison counts made in two or more separate areas. Accountability in the production department overlaps with accountability in inventory and storage (see previous chapter).

Production thefts occur primarily in two ways. Materials may be stolen outright by employees working in production, or diverted through the use of fictitious requisitions.

Outright Thefts

Individual theft losses are usually not large, because one man can conceal and carry out only a small quantity at one time. Effective physical security measures can usually prevent an employee from throwing material over a fence to be picked up later, or from being able to go to his car to conceal items during working hours. The real danger comes, then, from allowing employees free access to valuable material. An example will illustrate this danger.

An appliance manufacturer who used large quantities of copper wire never had any scrap wire to sell. The wiring department did not even have a container for scrap wire. Investigation showed that each employee carried his own scrap out each night in his pockets and lunch box. These scraps were purchased at full value by a local scrap dealer. Each man made 50 to 75 cents a day this way. They called it their "beer money." If the men did not produce enough scrap wire in normal operations, they simply cut up some good wire into scrap lengths. They made sure they got their "beer money" every day.

This may seem a small matter from the standpoint of dollar loss, but it grows in seriousness when 30 employees are doing it. In addition, such a practice induces a general dishonesty pattern. As outlined in the preceding chapter, proper accountability will indicate when production is requisitioning more of any item than normal production warrants. Particular attention should be paid to items that are especially tempting to thieves.

Diversion by Requisition

As stated before, accountability will not detect commercial quantity thefts in production areas as soon as they happen. Most losses will eventually show up in over-use of materials in production. But some additional security, some method of localizing when and where the loss occurred, is needed.

The production department is not the only area where requisitions can be used to accomplish diversion. A fictitious requisition could be used by the storeroom to account for material received short on a purchase kickback scheme. Or a fictitious requisition may release material from the storeroom to be sold by the thief.

In one case, a shortage was discovered when material no longer used in production was ordered sent back to the supplier for credit. The material was not in the storeroom. Its loss was traced back about 60 days to a fictitious requisition calling for return of the material for credit. The supplier said he had no record of the return and could not be proved to have received it. Requisition procedures made it impossible to assign responsibility for preparation of the fictitious requisition. No one remembered who hauled the material away.

Requisition Accountability

Everything removed from a storeroom should be authorized by a requisition. We are mainly concerned here with requisitions for production use, but the same system should guard all requisitions.

The requisition should be at least a three-part form. It need not be prenumbered. It will be prepared by the production unit that will use the material. All copies go first to an authorizing foreman or supervisor for his signature. He keeps one copy for his own records; the other two go to the storeroom. The storeroom fills the requisition and keeps one copy. The last copy goes back with the material to the production unit that made out the form.

The form serves both business and security needs in this path. It is filled out with the date, production department originating it, quantity and description of the material needed. The person who prepares it must initial it. It then goes to the supervisor, who signs it and keeps one copy.

The storeroom either fills it from stock on hand or uses it as the basis for preparing a purchase requisition. The storekeeper puts his name and the date on the form, keeps one copy and returns the other copy with the material to the production unit. If it is used as the basis for a purchase requisition, the storeroom keeps both copies. One is attached to the purchase requisition form copy retained by the storeroom. The other copy is retained in the storeroom until the material is received. Then it is completed and goes back to its point of origin with the requested material. This simple example can be expanded to meet more complex purchase procedures.

In this process security has three points for comparison: storeroom, production supervisor, and production unit. A missing copy in any of these places or any alteration on any copy should be investigated immediately.

Verification in Production Department

Production flow quantities discussed in the preceding chapter usually meet up with requisition quantities in the office of the production supervisor. Security can make its comparisons there while checking production flow quantities.

The limited availability of production material for theft should not eliminate security here. Accountability requires that production flow quantities be verified in the production department. That occasion should be used to make the extra security check of requisition verification.

CASE HISTORY #12

One Arctura Corporation storeroom contained only rolls of corrugated paper, sealing tape and related products from which shipping cartons were made. No requisitions were required for withdrawals of these items, because of their bulk and low value. For the same reason the receiving clerk made no actual count of these materials when he received them. He merely copied the quantities from the packing slip onto his receiving tally.

A storeroom clerk was a brother of the truck driver who usually delivered the box-making materials to Arctura. The brothers worked out a scheme whereby some of this material was sold for cash, at a reduced price, to a nearby small company. Most loads delivered to Arctura were short some items.

Some new accountability procedures went into effect in all of Arctura's storerooms after a security survey. When these new procedures were instituted, the truck driver's brother quit his job without reason. Because it appeared that the new procedures might have some connection with the resignation, security started an investigation. They found the diversion scheme.

QUESTION

What two basic accountability procedures for storerooms, recommended by the security survey, could have caused the brother in the storeroom to fear that his diversions were known and could no longer continue?

Chapter 14

Preventing Thefts in Sales

Employees can steal and sell whatever their employer manufactures. They can sell it for less than the company charges . . . after all, it didn't cost them anything to produce. Sales records also provide a tempting opportunity for massive employee thefts. Accountability ensures that the company receives payment for the goods it produces.

Importance of Sales Records

A company's manufacturing efforts all come together in one or more finished products which are ready to be sold. The company hopes to receive money in exchange for the products to keep the business going and make a profit. It is vital for the company to make sure it is receiving all the money paid for its products. If no accountability system is in effect, it is reasonably certain that some of the employees will be selling some of the merchandise for their own profit.

The author first developed the concept of accountability as a security system while conducting a group of security surveys for a national company. Their manufacturing plants produced one basic finished product in several sizes and finishes. It could be used for many purposes without further processing. Their processing plants also turned some of these finished products into structural parts for other companies. There were also independent processors doing the same thing. Thus, this company made one basic product with market value both as a finished product and as a raw material for further manufacturing. The company's executive office was in a city separate from its manufacturing plants. The executive office did all billing for the plants.

The original problem that led this company to seek help was loss of finished product. Company salesmen found their finished product in sales outlets that had never purchased anything from them. Quantities on sale at these outlets indicated thefts in truckload lots. Since the individual products were not worth very much in their present condition, it seemed likely that large quantities were involved. The geographic locations of these outlets would have made delivery of small quantities more costly than the products' value as stolen material.

Interlocking Forms

In illustrating how accountability is obtained, it is necessary to use interlocking forms reporting quantities. A fully operating system for sales orders requires using some forms from order filling and shipping departments. This chapter and the following one on shipping cannot be completely separated here. Accountability for one of these departments involves forms used in the other department. Illustrations of problems and solutions concerning sales order accountability will therefore mention shipping forms.

Stolen Market Values

Finished product diverted in small quantities for local sale suffers a great depreciation in value simply because it is stolen. The high risks run by the local sales outlet can only be counterbalanced by high profit. Product diverted in truckload quantities does not suffer as much depreciation. The thief usually bypasses one or more merchandising levels in finding a market. Sometimes the market even comes to him; he often steals on order.

The buyer gets material he already knows he can sell. This ensures the thief a higher return.

There are many profitable markets for various types of stolen goods. Stolen appliances may go on the shelf in a retail store. Wood paneling may go to a cash-and-carry outlet. Plumbing and electrical supplies may go directly into a new office building. Central heating and air conditioning units may go directly into new apartment or home construction.

With these types of markets for the stolen finished product, the employee thief may receive almost as much in stolen value as the manufacturer gets at wholesale value. The buyers' profits at this price and sales level are usually large enough to compensate for the risks involved.

Most urban centers now have some sort of "warehouse" outlet that provides another good way to dispose of stolen property. These outlets handle legitimate factory closeouts and bankrupt stocks; known and unknown brands are mixed together. Stolen and legitimately purchased material of the same brand may be mixed on the same shelf. The market for stolen property is there.

Receiving Sales Orders

Sales orders come from many sources, in many forms. Salesmen mail in orders daily as they travel their territories. They telephone in special or rush orders. They bring in orders when they return to the office. Customers familiar with the product may mail or telephone orders directly. Large customers and branch offices may send in orders by teletype.

Employees who take the initial action on orders from these diverse sources must sign each order. It is important for the sake of accountability to identify the person responsible for starting each order on its path toward shipment. This is particularly important on telephone orders, since processing of these orders starts before any confirmation from the customer. There is no proof of origin of a telephone order unless it is signed by the order taker. A diversion scheme being worked at this point needs a customer's name but not his permission. The company must be able to fix responsibility at every point where employees could cause product loss in commercial quantities. The sales order is one of those points.

Preliminary sales orders are not yet accepted orders. They may be made on a variety of forms and often come in single copies. They should be treated as preliminary orders only. No order filling or shipping should be done on the basis of a preliminary order alone. Recorded accountability starts only when preliminary orders are accepted for shipment.

Tight security at this point may require recording all preliminary orders before screening. This would not be a serious problem if the finished product comes in only a few standard types and sizes, or if sales are to a few large customers only. Whatever screening was necessary could be done after recording. The decisive factor here is cost. If a large number of recorded preliminary orders later have to be canceled, the cost could be high. The clerical cost of recording orders and then canceling them is wasted. There is also the added cost of having security check all canceled preliminary orders.

The decision can be based on knowledge of the percentage of total preliminary orders which are not accepted for shipment. The costs of recording can be weighed against the losses which can be prevented by recording.

Screening orders before recording them is the more widely used procedure. Elements of accountability can be present in either procedure.

Screening Sales Orders

All sales orders from all sources must go to a coordinator in the sales order department without delay. This can best be accomplished by having all preliminary orders, except mail orders, received in the sales order department. This includes telephone and teletype orders and those that salesmen bring in.

The coordinator should be well informed about products, prices and customers. He will be the best qualified employee to handle all telephone calls from customers, including those that result in orders. Mail orders should be sent to a coordinator directly — not by regular office messengers in their routine rounds. Security and good customer service require fast, direct delivery to the coordinator.

The coordinator's functions will include checking price, customer credit standing and merchandise availability. Coordinators will match confirming orders with phone orders already being processed. They will test the order and the customer by some pre-established criteria. One coordinator should do all the required screening on one order. Orders should not ordinarily leave the coordinator's possession until he has approved or disapproved them. (A special provision for abnormal delays in screening will be detailed later.)

Sales orders are the beginning of the final step in turning the finished product into money. They are "almost money" and should receive the protection their value warrants.

If the screening process rejects the preliminary sales order before recording, no entry has been made in any accountability record. Nothing has to be undone or canceled. If an order is rejected after recording, an accountability record must be canceled. This can take the form of a notice to the customer, with one copy going to the order recording clerk. The recording of the original approved order in the order register book is marked "canceled." The clerk who makes this entry notes it on the canceling form and initials the entry. The preliminary order and the canceling form then are filed together in an inactive customer file.

When an unrecorded preliminary order passes all screening tests, the coordinator notes this acceptance on the order and signs the acceptance. If he contacts other departments about this approval, a record should be made of the persons he consulted. This recording of responsibility tends to improve the quality of responsibility.

Time Limits on Orders

Each preliminary sales order should clear its coordinator within a prescribed time period. Constant pressure should be placed on accomplishing coordination within this time limit.

This requires close supervision within the sales order department. A cut-off time should also be set so coordinators receive no new, regular, preliminary sales orders after some time around 2:00 p.m. This cut-off allows coordinators to complete their screening and get all approved orders recorded that day.

Any orders received after the cut-off time are treated as next-day orders. They should be locked up overnight by a supervisor.

The cut-off time ensures that all accepted preliminary sales orders are recorded the same day they are received. No unrecorded orders should be in the possession of a coordinator or order clerk overnight. This is a strict requirement for good security.

Orders from all sources which are received after the cut-off time will be processed by coordinators first thing the following day. They can do this while waiting for the morning mail orders to reach them.

A simple way to achieve expeditious handling of preliminary orders with reduced supervision is to use timed clock stamps. Each station will stamp the date and time on the back of each preliminary order as it is received. Each station can be identified by a different color of stamp ink. The last stamping station will be the order recording clerk. The stamping causes no loss of time in processing. This or any other similar system should be inspected regularly by security, for two purposes: to see that all orders are processed to recording the same day received, and to make sure the processing was expeditious.

Bypassing the System

The coordinator is the only person in the normal routine who can legitimately change an order before recording. He can, therefore, make changes for his own profit without being noticed. Coordinators can bypass part of the system if accountability is not well established.

Example: A coordinator held out a friend's order so it was not recorded. He came back at night and assigned it a sales order number previously assigned to another order by the order clerk. He then mixed this unrecorded preliminary order with the recorded, untyped orders left over at the close of business. The next day the typist started it on its way to be filled and shipped. The coordinator then asked the order filling and shipping departments to return all tally and completed order copies directly to him. He played on their sympathy by saying he had made an error and wanted to correct it before it was caught. He destroyed all order and tally copies, including the billing copy, as he received them. His friend received a truckload of merchandise he did not have to pay for.

There are good business reasons for not letting coordinators keep unrecorded orders overnight. They might lose them or forget what processing has been done. They may miss a function or waste time repeating one that has already been completed. The added security risks make this practice prohibitive. No unrecorded orders should be available to coordinators or order clerks at the close of the day's business.

Screening Deviations

Some legitimate delays may prevent same-day order processing and recording. The coordinator must send these delayed preliminary orders to the order record clerk. The clerk will assign each a sales order number, record other identifying data and return it to the coordinator. The order record book will also show that the preliminary order went back to the coordinator untyped. Security will follow each of these deviations to ensure their proper completion and disposition.

Allowing any deviation in normal procedure opens a door to the dishonest person. If the accountability system is effective and practical, true deviations should be rare. Each deviation should be questioned by security. The reason for the deviation should be verified and the person calling for the deviation should be recorded. Any increase in the number of deviations will be a danger signal to security. An increase in deviations by any one person will usually indicate dishonesty or lack of ability.

Either case requires special attention from security.

Recording Sales Orders

The recording clerk's duties do not include making any decisions. The clerk records action taken by others. While he exercises no control over these actions, the clerk's recording of them is the primary accountability station in sales order handling.

The recording clerk's first function is to assign sales order numbers serially as the orders arrive. One successful method is a bound book where the numbers run serially down the lefthand margin. These can be handwritten numbers as long as their numerical sequence is checked. Opposite the assigned number the order recording clerk enters the customer's name and the date the clerk received the order. The order number is entered on the preliminary order.

The preliminary orders, with assigned numbers and other information from coordinator screening, go to a typist who types them on permanent sales order forms. The number of copies made does not concern security as long as all copies are legible. These do not need to be prenumbered forms; the sales order register book serves that purpose. One copy should, however, be filed numerically in the sales order department to help prevent duplicate use of a number.

Distribution of Sales Order Copies

After the sales order is typed it should be checked against the preliminary order for accuracy and completeness.

The sales order department should keep one copy, with the preliminary order attached, in an unfilled order file. Other copies will be distributed as required by the company's gathering and shipping procedures. If billing is done in another location, one copy of the order can go there to assist in later invoice preparation. If billing is done at the shipping point, this copy is not needed.

Accountability Points

Other copies of the sales order can be fed back to the sales order register from any place where accountability points are needed. For example, order filling can send a copy back on completion of its function. The date the order was filled would then be entered in the sales order register book. This would catch a duplicate use of an order number or the filling of an order without a number.

When ordered products are gathered for shipment, a shipping tally will be made without access to a copy of the sales order. The tally will go to shipping with the gathered products and will be verified there as the products are prepared for shipment. There the date shipped and the bill of lading number will be added to the tally. Two copies of the tally then go to the order clerk if billing is done in another location. The order clerk enters the date shipped and the bill of lading number in the order register book. These should be the next-to-last entries opposite the sales order number. The clerk notes on both tally copies that these entries have been made. One tally copy is sent to the billing location by the order clerk as proof of shipping for billing purposes.

The order filling and shipping functions are condensed here to avoid confusion with the sales order process. Filling and shipping will be covered specifically in the next chapter. It should be noted again that accountability in either sales order handling or in shipping requires use of forms from the other function. An accountability form flow chart for both sales order preparation and shipping is included in the next chapter.

The preliminary order and its typed copy are pulled from the unfilled order file when shipment is reported. The order clerk's second copy of the shipping tally is attached to them. This makes up a completed order package. It is filed in an inactive customer file if billing is done in another location.

If shipping and billing are done at the same location, only one copy of the tally will go to the order clerk. Then the completed order package will go to accounts receivable for billing.

Regardless of where the invoice is prepared, a copy should go to the order clerk. The date billed is then the last entry in the order register book for each order number where no back orders are required. This invoice copy is then filed in the completed order package.

Accountability can be obtained through just these order register book entries. The sales order number appears on the order, tally copy, bills of lading and invoices. All can be checked against each other and against entries in the order register book. The customer's name in the register book leads to the inactive customer file, containing a copy of the typed order, preliminary order, tally and invoice. These various forms can be compared and any deviation in quantity or price should be referred to security.

The sales order register book entries must be complete. Dates and numbers entered in the register must agree with the forms in the inactive customer file.

This system provides security with a wide variety of check-points. Security can vary what it checks so that no employee can take advantage of any gaps without considerable risk. Spot checking will usually suffice until deviations are noted.

All of these records lead back to the sales order register book, which in turn leads to all other required records. Accountability depends on the accuracy of the entries in this register. These entries should be verified as often as necessary to keep them accurate. Any errors or omissions must be called to the attention of the responsible employee and his supervisor.

An Inadequate System

An unchecked sales order register book provides no security by itself. In the manufacturing company in which the author first developed accountability as a security system, a sales order register book was used, but no entries were ever verified back to the original sources. The register was used merely to show what order number came next, even though there were spaces for other entries. Even its use for this purpose was subject to question.

Each month this order register book had one or two numbers with nothing recorded after them. No information was ever located for some of these numbers. There was no way of checking back to verify if the numbers were actually used at all.

The billing office, in another city, received a copy of each typed sales order. It then received teletypes listing completed orders. This was their signal to issue invoices. At the end of each month, the uncompleted order copies over a certain age were thrown away. They were presumed to have been canceled, issued in error or superseded by change orders. Their uncompleted status was never verified.

A coordinator at the manufacturing plant could ask for an order number but hold the preliminary order on his desk. Days later he could take the preliminary order directly to the typist. She would type up a sales order, complete with an order number that had never been entered in the order register book. The shipping copy of the sales order and other copies were destroyed after the order was filled. The billing office was never notified to prepare an invoice. Eventually its copy of the sales order was thrown away. A carload or a truckload of finished product was shipped without record or billing. A vacant line following an order number was the only record.

Back Orders

Some sales orders will not be filled completely in one shipment. In this case, the original sales order should not remain open awaiting further shipment. The order filling department should fill out a back order form showing what was not shipped, plus order identifying data. This should go with copies of the tally through the shipping department to the sales order department. It should be a prenumbered form with the usual one copy filed numerically where prepared. Two other copies would go with the tally.

When the coordinator receives these back order forms, he should compare them with the tally and original order. If quantities and other information are correct, he approves the back order as though it were a new preliminary order. The order clerk gets this approved back order copy and records it as a new order in the order register book with the back order number as an added entry.

The coordinator attaches the other back order copy to the completed order package and sends this package to the order clerk. This clerk uses the package to record the completed order number on the new back order entry in the register book. The new number is then entered on the completed order package. Thus the register book shows the new order originating from the old order, and the old order closed out by the new order. This allows the original order and all its back orders to be checked backward or forward with full continuity. This back order system is followed until the original order is completely shipped.

If the complete order is canceled at any point after being typed, all copies of all forms prepared up to the time of cancellation (except those filed in the numerical files) must be included in the completed order package before it is filed. This will prevent misuse of any parts of these forms. Partial cancellation is not of interest to security as long as the billing matches the tally and shipping copies in quantity. Security can compare these in audits of the completed order packages.

The back order numerical file will allow security to verify that each one was recorded in the order register book. After that verification the back order is treated as another sales order by security.

Accountability for sales orders does not require any forms that are not already prepared for normal business use. It may sometimes require more copies of some of these forms. Preparation of extra copies usually presents no problems, nor does it add appreciable cost.

Sales Order Flow

Figure 3 overlaps a similar chart at the end of the next chapter on accountability in shipping. Order filling and shipping are condensed in this sales order flow chart. The sales order handling is condensed in the shipping chart.

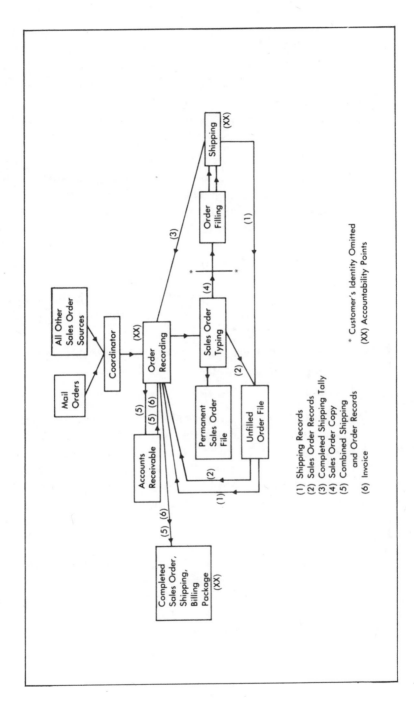

(1) Shipping Records
(2) Sales Order Records
(3) Completed Shipping Tally
(4) Sales Order Copy
(5) Combined Shipping
    and Order Records
(6) Invoice

* Customer's Identity Omitted
(XX) Accountability Points

Figure 3. Sales Order Flow

The order recording operation is the center of the sales order flow system. Sales orders go from recording to typing, with at least four typed copies going to the following places, as shown in Figure 3:

1. One to the permanent sales order file in the sales order department to record complete number sequence.

2. One to the unfilled order file in the sales order department where it remains until shipping records show shipment on the order. Then, with the shipping records, it goes back to the order recording clerk. That clerk makes entries showing bill of lading number. These shipping records will contain the order number, customer's name and quantities shipped and back ordered. These should agree with order number, customer's name and quantities ordered on the copy of the sales order from the unfilled order file in the sales order department.

3. The order filler gets one copy that does not show the customer's name or address.

4. The last copy goes to the traffic department.

Order filling and shipping are shown here only to illustrate their interlocking accountability use. Order filling sends at least two copies of each filled order list to shipping. Shipping then sends one copy as a shipping tally to the order recording clerk containing bill of lading number and date shipped. The other shipping tally copy goes with all shipping records to be matched up with the unfilled order copy, and then is sent on to the order recording clerk.

After all required recording, the order record clerk sends the complete package to accounts receivable for billing. The package then goes back to the recording clerk for recording of invoice date and number. This entire package is then filed as the complete sales order package.

CASE HISTORY #13

The Arctura Corporation's sales order record book was a blank bound book with sales order numbers written in serially on the lefthand side as orders were entered. The only other information entered in the book was the customer's name and his order number, and the date the order was shipped. No security use was made of this order register.

Prior to the time of the security survey, a salesman noted that a retail unit about a hundred miles from the plant had a new Arctura product on sale that he knew had not yet been released for sale. The factory advised him that they had no record of having sold or shipped any. Someone had diverted a quantity of this new product before it was even announced publicly.

An outside investigation showed at least one truckload had been taken out of the plant. Arctura did not want the embarrassment of trying to find out how the dealer obtained this stolen merchandise. But the incident moved the company to have a complete security survey made and to institute some accountability security measures.

An investigation at Arctura verified that all fully entered orders in the order register book at about the date of this diversion were legitimate orders that were shipped and billed. But there was one order number skipped completely in the listing; 2893 followed 2891. There were also two instances where numbers were entered in the book but had nothing else filled in. One of these numbers was found to belong to an order that one of the coordinators was holding until the ordered material was in stock. No record was ever found for the other entered number.

Coordinated records were so poor that it was considered impossible to determine from records just how the diverted merchandise left the plant.

QUESTIONS

1. What was the primary error in the handling of sales orders that permitted this diversion?
2. What should the minimum entry in the sales order register contain before an order can be cleared for filling and shipping?
3. What is the last item entered in the sales order register?
4. What is the most important accountability point in the sales order flow system?

Chapter 15

How to Isolate Shipping Losses

There are three basic requirements for security in the shipping process:

1. An order filler must not know whose order he is filling.
2. The shipping department must not have access to the stockroom.
3. Bills of lading must not be prepared in the shipping department.

This isolation is necessary for accountability to prevent temptation and is a company's best protection against employee dishonesty.

When Shipping Begins

A sales order is simply a list of the quantities of finished products that a customer has agreed to buy. The sales order authorizes surrender of the products to the customer for a specified sum of money. All the other terms and specifications on the order form merely define how, when and where the surrender occurs.

The shipping process begins when the sales order begins to change from a list of products into the products themselves. By this time, all approval and screening action on the order is complete, and conversion begins. The conversion process really starts when the order filling section receives one or more copies of the sales order.

Deletion of Customer's Name

Accountability requires a major deletion from the sales order information when the sales order goes to the order filling section. The order filler must not know the name and address of the customer. He does not need this information to perform his duties. His possession of the customer name and address can only lead to confusion or misuse.

The sales order number provides the best means of sales order identification. Using the customer's name for identifying an order can be confusing. One customer may have more than one order in process; a customer with many branches may have many orders being filled at the same time. A sales order number is anonymous and carries its own identity; the name confusion is eliminated. The number also eliminates the temptation for employees to give a favored customer free products or to set up diversion schemes for their own profit.

It is easy for an order filler to overfill a standard package and bypass any checking done by the shipping clerk. Collusion between filler and shipper will materially increase the quantity of these losses.

Good business practice and accountability are served by elimination of customer name and address at this point. The customer's identity should not be revealed until the order is packed for shipment.

Order Filling

Numbers become increasingly important as inventories are automated. Product names, colors, styles, sizes and location are translated into numbers to assist machine accounting. These numbers tend to reduce error in order filling because they reduce the need for personal judgment. A four- or five-digit number can indicate product, color, style and size. All the filler then needs to submit to his judgment is quantity, storage location, and delivery location in the shipping department. Storage and delivery locations may also be coded, leaving quantity as the only important judgment variable.

This coding is instituted for accounting purposes. It can be used to reduce human error in order filling. It also isolates employees from information they need to derive a dishonest profit. Order fillers do not need to know who gets the shipment, and they should not know. Keeping this information from them helps provide accountability.

There are many small companies where inventory coding is not practical. Minimum security still requires that the customer name and address be withheld from the order filler. The person writing up the sales order prepares two copies, showing only order number, quantity, description, and delivery location. The order filler gathers the required items and delivers them, with these forms completed, to the shipping department.

The shipping clerk checks the gathered material against the quantities and descriptions on the order filling form, and signs the form. The form then becomes the shipping tally. The clerk packs the material for shipment and places the sales order number on each package. He indicates the number of packages, weight and other necessary information on the tally.

Isolation Provides Accountability

The shipping clerk sends a copy of the completed tally to the traffic office, where a bill of lading is prepared. Copies of the bill of lading and a copy of the sales order containing customer name and address go back to shipping so that shipment can be completed as ordered. After shipment, all remaining forms are returned to the sales order department, where they are matched with the sales order copy in the unfilled order file. Comparison of these forms will reveal any deviation. If no deviations are found, all the shipping and sales order forms go to accounting for billing. The shipping function has provided two independent counts: by the filler and by the shipping clerk. The customer's identity is not known by the persons making these counts.

This isolation can be accomplished in a company of any size by following these rules:

1. The order filler is never given the customer's name.
2. The order filler does no shipping.
3. The shipping clerk does no order filling.
4. The shipping clerk provides a shipping tally before learning the customer's identity.
5. The stockroom and shipping areas must be separated.

Larger companies will have more complex systems. This is partly because of size alone, and partly because of a larger variety of finished products. More than one order filler may assemble products on one order. The following is one illustration of procedures in a larger shipping department.

Sample Shipping Procedures

As an example, let us examine one company's order filling and shipping methods. In this sample company, when the order filling department receives a sales order, the clerks code each item according to classes of products ordered and warehouse locations. Various locations in the warehouse are identified by different colors of order filling cards. Identifying data not needed by the order filler is punched, but not printed, on the card.

Each order filler gets the color of card that designates his particular warehouse area. The information printed on the card tells him only the item number, quantity ordered, and shipping dock location where he is to leave the material he gathers. After doing what each card instructs, he initials and time stamps it. He turns in the completed cards as he picks up his next batch of cards. The process is completely impersonal.

When all cards on one order have been completed and

turned in, the shipping and traffic departments are notified. Notification is made by other copies of the sales order that contain all information except the customer's identity. The shipping copy is verified by having the shipping department check material on the dock with information on the sales order. Shipping then signs the sales order copy so it becomes a shipping tally.

If shipping finds anything wrong in quantity or quality, it notifies the order filling section. It is the responsibility of order filling to verify the difference and correct it. This is accomplished by having shipping prepare a simple shipping difference form for order filling use, with one copy going to the security department. When order filling makes the necessary correction, it notes that change on the form and returns it to shipping.

Security uses these shipping difference forms for two purposes. A complete investigation is made if the difference indicates a possible product diversion attempt. Differences caused by human error or carelessness are recorded for future reference. If these errors form a pattern needing correction, remedial measures are recommended by security.

It is worth emphasis here that this company did not allow the shipping department to go to a stockroom to correct an error. This system was set up after discovering that the shipping department regularly went into the stockroom whether shipping errors existed or not. The shipping employees kept their friends well-stocked with material for which no one was ever billed.

In the accountability system, shipping verifies that the order filling form matches the material delivered to it for shipment. It signs the form, which then becomes the shipping tally. This goes to the traffic department with all information about packages and weights needed for preparation of the bill of lading. Traffic will already have received a complete copy of the sales order from the order typist. Traffic compares this with the shipping tally and prepares the bill of lading. The bill of lading and the complete sales order copy then go to shipping as final authority to ship.

In some systems, the sales order is prepared in sufficient copies so that no new forms are needed throughout the order filling and shipping process, up to the preparation of the bill of lading. One copy can even be used as part of the gate pass for truck shipments. Multiple use of one form reduces chance of error and saves time and money in forms preparation.

Bills of Lading

Bills of lading should not be prepared in the shipping department. Shipping should not know the purchaser's name until it receives the bill of lading. Most companies have a traffic department or employees who perform that function. That department should receive a completed copy of the typed sales order. This will match up with the sales order number on the shipping tally. The bill of lading is prepared and sent back to shipping as final authority to ship. Shipping sometimes needs to know the method of shipment for packing purposes before receiving the bill of lading. This can be included on the order filling form which the shipping department receives with the material from the order filler. This does not increase security risks.

The bill of lading is another prenumbered form, with one copy filed numerically where prepared. Other copies go to shipping for use in making rail and truck line shipments.

Truck Shipments

On all truck shipments requiring bills of lading, the trucks picking up shipments should enter and leave the plant by one specified gate. Each driver must give the gate guard two things before leaving the gate: a shipping tally copy and a bill of lading copy. The shipping tally copy will show the number of shipping packages making up the order. The gate guard will compare the quantity of packages on the truck, on the shipping tally and on the bill of lading. They must agree before the truck is permitted to leave.

If these forms do not agree, a high level plant supervisor must go to the gate and clear up the discrepancy. This supervisor should not be from the sales order preparation, filling or shipping departments. He should be someone with enough authority to cure the causes of the differences in any of these departments.

This point is very important for two reasons. First is the inherent danger in permitting errors to go uncorrected. Small differences become big differences; occasional errors become frequent ones. Temptation increases as the rate and size of differences increase. The second reason is the increased difficulty of pinpointing causes of errors after the truck and shipment are gone. Was it a clerical error? Was the order intentionally overfilled? Were two different shipments mixed up in loading? Is the truck driver picking up something on the way out?

There is also a management reason for having a high official make these corrections. If he is called away from his primary responsibilities very often to clear up discrepancies, his performance of those important functions will decline and he will soon correct the bothersome shipping problems.

If the gate guard finds that the truckload and both forms agree, he lets the truck pass after collecting one copy each of the tally and bill of lading. These copies are generally used thereafter for some normal business function. The gate guard will have logged each truck as it entered. He completes these log entries by showing time out, order number, customer's name and bill of lading number on each order.

This log is the final shipping accountability record. Security will check its entries regularly against the sales order register entries of the same information. These entries should agree exactly, except for the shipping date. The date of the bill of lading, entered in the register, may be a day or two earlier than actual shipment. This date spread should not be permitted to grow beyond reasonable limits.

Proper security use of this truck gate log will also prevent duplicate use of order and bill of lading numbers. Any attempt at duplicate use should be investigated by security.

Truckload shipments to one customer can also be handled in the same manner as rail car shipments described below, including use of a numbered door seal and a request for its number verification on the receiving end.

Rail Shipments

Shipment by rail boxcar does not allow use of the gate guard as one step in security. These cars should be tallied when loaded just like truck shipments. An additional entry on all copies of the tally will be the car seal numbers.

Railroads provide seals in quantity with continuous number series. The security department should obtain these seals and keep them locked up until they are needed. There are several relatively safe ways to control their issuance. As a general rule, shipping can ask security for two seals for each rail car. They will be issued in recorded, serially numbered groups for whatever cars are going to be completely loaded each day. Any seals not used by the end of the day should be returned to security. Unused seals should never be left out overnight.

As a rule, a gate guard will open rail gates to let switch engines into the plant area. He can report the number of empty boxcars coming into the yard. Security can keep a running tally of empty cars entering and car seals issued. All broken or damaged seals should be returned to security as their own authorization for replacement. Damaged seals should be checked back against the current number series before they are replaced.

The shipping tally copies should all show the numbers of the two car seals used on that recorded shipment. One copy of this tally should be placed in a sealed envelope in the car as a packing list.

Any complaints from customers about shortages or differences should list the car seal numbers. The packing list in the car should contain prominent notice of this requirement. There is another good security reason for listing seal numbers on packing slips — accountability.

Example: In one instance the shipping foreman kept several hundred car seals in a box on his office floor. Anyone who needed car seals simply came in and helped himself. Prior to the security survey, the loading crew went to the stockroom to pick up whatever was short on a shipment without any record being made of what, or how much, material they took. On some of these trips they picked up material not called for on the order and placed it on top of the order in the car. When they picked up car seals for the car they also picked up one or more extra seals.

The loaded, sealed rail cars were taken outside the fence to be picked up by the train crews that night. The employees with the extra seals would then get to the car before the train crews made their pickup. They would break a seal, take out the extra material and reseal the car with one of the extra seals. There was nothing to alert anyone to wrongdoing; the shipment was received without shortage. The car arrived with unbroken seals. But the inventory shortage got larger each month.

Accountability on rail car shipments does not have the help of the gate guard that is present on truck shipments. An additional step is therefore needed on a spot basis — a check that the car has the same numbered seals when it reaches its destination as it had when it left the plant. This can be accomplished by use of a postage-paid reply card placed in the sealed packing list envelope in the car. It will have the order number on it, and two blank spaces for the numbers of the car seals on the car when it arrives at its destination. The return address on the card will be a box number used by the security department. The customer will be asked to write in the seal numbers and mail the card back.

For a number of reasons, usually no more than half the cards will be returned. Accountability will be maintained, however, because employees cannot know which cards will be returned. Moreover, shipping employees will know that this procedure is followed. It will be another step to reduce temptation and induce greater honesty.

Customer Pickup

There will be no bill of lading if a customer picks up his own shipment. He should use the truck gate so he can be logged in and out. The traffic department merely uses a will-call form in place of a bill of lading form. These should be prenumbered forms used in the same fashion as bills of lading. Accountability handling will be the same as if they were bills of lading.

Miscellaneous Shipments

If the company ships by its own trucks, there will be no bill of lading. A company may use a different type of order form when shipping to its own distribution centers. There are many variations of shipping systems that can provide complete accountability. Security can adjust to any system if they are familiar with it.

Even for intra-company shipments, it must be kept in mind that accountability requires that material counts be verified by a second, independent count. As we have learned, this is accomplished by a simple process in shipping: the order filler should not know whose order he is filling, and the shipping employees should not be allowed into the stockroom. This is just as important in shipping to branches as it is in shipping to outside customers.

The other protective procedures mentioned simply reinforce these two rules. Again, all of this protection is generally obtained by use of existing forms and practices, thereby adding little to costs. This extra security should be obtained wherever possible.

Cash Sales

Most of the accountability procedures applied in this chapter concern formal, written orders. Many manufacturers have sales areas where local users of their products can buy small quantities for cash, without a written order.

There are many businesses and branch operations where one person is permitted to receive cash from such sales and make out the receipt. A city cash counter often uses a cash drawer instead of a cash register. This is an open invitation to steal. The temptation would seem to be so obvious that correction would be almost automatic.

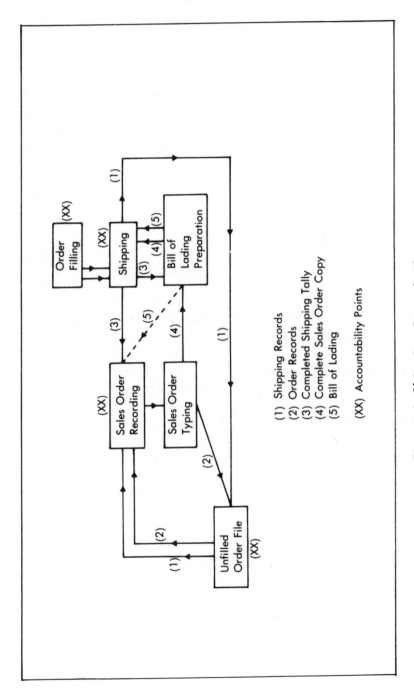

(1) Shipping Records
(2) Order Records
(3) Completed Shipping Tally
(4) Complete Sales Order Copy
(5) Bill of Lading

(XX) Accountability Points

Figure 4. Shipping Records Flow

Correction calls only for accountability. The seller should not handle the cash payment. A numbered sales slip should be written up for each sale. One copy will remain in the sales area. The other copy should bear the imprint of the cash register where the money was received. The accounting department then needs only to run a tape on the copies in the sales area, verify the total with the total in the cash register, and be sure that all numbered copies are accounted for.

Shipping Records Flow

The chart in Figure 4 is an expansion of the shipping section of the chart in Figure 3 in the preceding chapter. Accountability overlaps here so that neither chapter is complete in itself. The sales order section of Figure 4 is condensed. The reader should refer back to the preceding chapter for details of the flow of sales orders into the shipping department.

Following this flow chart provides us with a summary of the shipping procedure. The order filler should not know the name and address of the customer. The order filling department sends at least two copies of the filled sales order form to the shipping department. The material delivered there by the order filler is checked against these forms. The shipping clerk signs these forms if they agree with the material delivered by order filling. These forms then become shipping tallies (3). One copy goes to the traffic department for bill of lading preparation. There it meets a complete copy of the sales order (4) previously sent to it when the sales order was typed.

The traffic department prepares a bill of lading or other shipping instruction form and sends it and the complete sales order form (4) (5) back to shipping as authority to ship. Further accountability can be obtained if desired by sending a copy of the bill of lading (5) direct from traffic to sales order recording.

The shipping department then sends a completed copy of the tally (3) to the sales order recording clerk, who enters bill of lading information and date shipped opposite the sales order number. Shipping then sends all shipping forms (1) to the sales order department where it meets the sales order records (2). The records then follow the paths previously charted and described in detail in the preceding Sales Records chapter.

The accountability points are the order recording clerk, shipping department, and the unfilled order file in the sales order department. The order filling operation can also be used as another accountability point if desired. The shipping function itself contains other points of accountability such as the gate guard, and car seals which guard against theft and diversion after the shipment leaves the shipping dock.

CASE HISTORY #14

Prior to the Arctura security survey, a copy of the complete sales order form was always sent from the typist to the order filler. He then filled the order and took it to the shipping dock where his copy of the sales order became the shipping tally and was used to prepare the bill of lading in the shipping department. Billing was done from another copy of the sales order form sent directly to the executive offices in another city when the sales order was typed up. Billing was done after receiving a teletype message each day listing the sales order numbers shipped that day by the factory.

The shipping department went directly to the storeroom to correct any errors made in filling the order.

The shipping department, over a period of years, became a family affair as the man in charge replaced resigning employees with his relatives. These family members started taking electric appliances out of the storeroom for their own use without paying for them. Finally one family member started a small retail appliance store. He bought some Arctura products through regular purchase orders, but he filled his shelves with other Arctura merchandise loaded on his truck as free extras by his relatives in the shipping department.

Accountability later put an end to this practice and the relative's appliance store went out of business when he had to start competing with larger stores on price.

QUESTIONS

1. At what point in sales order processing does shipping begin?
2. In what primary way was the shipping department allowed to avoid the rules of accountability?
3. How could accountability in the personnel department have helped prevent these losses through the shipping department?

Chapter 16

Accounting Department Accountability

Up to this point accountability has dealt with protection of materials that go through various processes from requisition to finished product. In this chapter we are concerned with money: the return from the finished product after it is sold, and the ways in which this return can also be stolen.

Money As A Commodity

Money represents raw material and labor transformed into a medium which can be exchanged for more raw material and labor to start more production. It is the perpetuating link between finished product and new raw materials. In this context it is a commodity that needs consideration in a security program. It becomes accountable property, subject to the same accountability rule as other property: quantities must constantly be verified by a second, independent count.

Dollar values influence temptation levels. Money itself therefore offers the highest level of temptation. It needs no conversion and suffers no loss in value when stolen.

Money is much easier to control than other commodities because it is subject to constant inventory. This is so because it is the commodity by which all other commodities are valued.

Business has always recognized the need for some accountability for money. The problem is that accounting places most of its emphasis on balancing accounts after the accounts are established. Little emphasis is placed on *how* the accounts are established, and how dissipated.

Most of the problem will be eliminated if the procedures for commodity accountability set out in prior chapters of this section are followed. Verified purchases will become verified finished product — sold, billed, and collected.

Account Manipulation

The remaining problems in money accountability involve conversion of money totally unrelated to commodity movement. These conversions take place within the accounting department by manipulation of accounting records. No outside collusion is required. One person in the right place with the right authority can steal with relative safety.

There have been many known instances of fictitious supply companies being set up, complete with stationery and bank account. An employee of the purchasing company with power to approve and pay invoices can set up such a scheme. Fictitious invoices are approved and paid. The checks go through the fictitious company bank account, and everything looks normal. The purchasing company employee involved files his fictitious records away, with no resulting inventory record or shortage of material.

Any system of accountability divides accounting authority so the person who approves payments cannot make the payments. The best security does not permit records of payments to be filed until an independent audit is made. This audit makes sure that copies of authentic purchase and receiving records support the payment.

Accountability must be adapted to a variety of circumstances to prevent money losses. Direct money losses occur in direct proportion to the availability of money. More currency on hand means more temptation to steal.

Losses of money are not confined to currency. Any business which receives payment for its product or service is vulnerable to diversion of those payments. Receipts can be diverted, just as payments for products or services can be diverted. Some examples will illustrate the nature of this threat.

Examples of Poor Money Accountability

In a newspaper office, one employee was permitted to receive currency from customers and make out bank deposits. Classified advertisements were taken over the phone without advance payment. It was impractical to set up an accounts receivable system for these small amounts. A statement was mailed for each one, and a carbon copy of the statement was the office record of the receivable. A tape was run on the unpaid total each week, but this was only for management information.

Many advertising payments were made in person at the newspaper office, often in currency. The employee who made out the bank deposits received many of these office payments. She deposited checks to the bank account but kept all the currency she received. She merely destroyed the office copy of the statement for each currency payment she pocketed. In two and a half years she had put over $7,500 of the newspaper's income into her own pocket.

In many isolated operations the paymaster can simply add a fictitious employee to the payroll and forge the signature on the check when it is received on the job. Each group foreman keeps a record of time for each of his employees. These are never compared with the payroll record turned in for payment by the supervisor. One person prepares the payroll and approves it for payment.

Another example concerns a small branch operation where the manager compiled and approved all payrolls. He arranged to record overtime for several employees who did not work the overtime. He split the extra money with these employees. Another time he recorded an hourly employee as working for two weeks when the employee had been absent on a personal trip. The manager and the absent employee split the extra money.

In another instance, the comptroller of a large corporation diverted $35,000 by account manipulation. The money was received by check as a rebate on workmen's compensation insurance expense. The premiums on this insurance had been paid in advance, based on a projection of the prior year's experience, and overpayment was rebated at year's end. The check was deposited to the general bank account of the insured company but was not credited as a reduction of insurance expense. The credit went to a "suspense account" with a strange title ("Miscellaneous Exchange") which did not identify the source of the credit.

This account was later closed out and the amount credited to another account whose title made it appear to be for engineering services accounts payable. About six months later, before the annual audit, the account was closed out by checks to individuals which were charged to engineering expense. The comptroller did all this manipulating of accounts, and signed the checks, all within the normal limits of his assigned duties. He changed a credit entry from a reduction of an expense into a liability.

Two by now familiar lessons can be drawn from these examples. First, one person should never be given authority to approve payments and also make payments. Secondly, accountability procedures should always independently verify all receipts and disbursements before their records are filed away.

CASE HISTORY #15

The Arctura Corporation operates a service parts center at the factory. It acts as a supplier of parts to local repairmen who service Arctura appliances. It sells for cash only. Sales are supposed to be written up on a register machine which provides an original receipt for the buyer and a carbon copy which stays in the machine.

At the end of each day the salesperson on duty adds up the total of all sales on the duplicates in the machine and turns in that same amount of cash from the cash drawer.

During the security survey it was noted that the service parts salesman asked each purchaser if he needed a receipt. He only wrote up sales on the register machine if a receipt was requested. All money seemed to go into the cash drawer, but that night the only cash turned in was what was called for by the receipt copies.

During the lunch hour the next day a supervisor from the accounting department was instructed to count the cash drawer and add up the receipt copies total. He found over $20 more in the cash drawer than the receipts called for.

The salesman on duty admitted that he was regularly taking $30 to $50 a day for himself for the sales he did not write up. All the money went into the cash drawer as he made sales. At day's end he added up the total of the duplicate sales tickets and turned in that amount of cash from the drawer. He then counted out the $15 cash that was left in the drawer for next day's change. Whatever money was left was his.

QUESTIONS

1. Why does money offer the highest level of temptation for theft?
2. How would accountability prevent the cash thefts described in this case?
3. What is the basic accountability rule in handling and accounting for cash?

Chapter 17

Accountability in Retail

Throughout this book, with its emphasis on removing temptation and reinforcing employee honesty through a system of accountability, examples have been drawn largely from a manufacturing system, and specifically a large production facility. Obviously the principles discussed can be modified or adapted to suit the smaller organization performing similar or identical functions. But those same principles apply with equal force to the retail operation, where internal theft continues to be a serious problem — perhaps *the* most serious problem in the average retail company's profit picture.

In general, operational accountability can be adapted to any business. Naturally there will be differences of emphasis and detail in the application of those procedures. Remember that there are two governing goals:

1. To employ relatively honest people, and
2. To keep them honest by making it difficult, dangerous and unprofitable to steal.

In designing an accountability system for a particular business of any kind, manufacturing or retail, every procedure must be measured against these basic purposes.

• In *hiring employees*, the retail organization should give the same concern to application forms and hiring policies that is detailed in Chapter 8, with the objective of finding relatively honest employees and screening out that 25 percent who are actively looking for ways to steal.

Because there is a relatively high turnover rate in many retail store operations, there will be a tendency to bypass some of the recommended hiring procedures, such as verification of the information sought on the application form and a credit check. It must be remembered, however, that each such reduction in accountability procedures carries with it an increase in risk.

• In *executive accountability*, the importance of care in selection and backgrounding is as obvious in retail as in manufacturing operations. The impact that an executive's performance has on the honesty of those who work under him underscores the necessity of seeing that relatively honest executives are hired in the first place, and that accountability procedures will encourage those executives to stay honest.

• In *purchasing*, the basic principles of accountability are vital to a successful retail operation. Here the company is not purchasing raw materials for the making of a new product, but buying the finished products themselves. The potential for kickback schemes, diversion of ordered products before delivery, pilferage and theft by employees for personal use or for resale, is at least as great as in the production phase, and the same techniques for assuring employee honesty apply. In particular, all purchasing must be done through a purchasing department, and all purchases must be verified as received, using the purchase order accountability practices outlined in Chapter 10.

• In *receiving*, such accountability procedures as verified counts, verified comparison of what was ordered with what was received, physical isolation of the receiving department, multiple distribution of the receiving tally form, etc., are equally essential in retail as in manufacturing operations. The procedures outlined in Chapter 11 are readily adapted to any business, retail or manufacturing, large or small.

• *Inventories* in a manufacturing operation are of both raw materials and finished products. Many of the former have, in their unfinished state, relatively little value for potential thieves. In retail situations, however, virtually everything is salable at a profit to the thief, and the potential for either small individual thefts or large-scale bulk thefts is, if anything, increased. The combination of frequent verified counts, requisition accountability as outlined in Chapter 12, and physical security measures for storerooms and warehouses will help to reduce temptation and encourage honesty. Accountability in receiving and shipping is, of course, fundamental to accountability in warehousing and storing. Where there is accurate, verified recording of everything received, and an accurate, verified record of everything removed from inventory, employees will be quick to recognize the hazards of attempting to divert products for their own use.

• The primary difference between *sales accountability* in retail and manufacturing operations rests in the fact that in the latter most sales are made by means of a sales order from an off-site destination, processed in a sales order department, while in retail stores most sales are made at the cash register in a particular sales department, whether the sale is of a carry-out item or one that must be delivered later.

Accountability demands that no product be delivered to a customer without a sales record; that sales records be prenumbered and traceable to the person making the sale; that all stock moving into and out of a department be verified by a record of that movement confirmed in more than one location; that in cash sales over the counter, all sales must be recorded on prenumbered sales slips, and the sales person should not be authorized to make cash sales unless the retained copy of the sales slip bears a cash register receipt imprint in the exact amount of the sale.

Clerks in most retail stores have registers capable of making such an imprint. It would not be practical in most retail stores to require clerks to take the money to a cashier or have the customer pay somewhere else. Discount type stores do have checkout counters, and some large department stores now use centralized cashiers, but in these instances the cashier takes the place of the sales clerk. So the same person records the sale and records the cash receipt; these cashiers have the same opportunities for theft that the counter sales clerk has.

Having the cash register imprint on the sales slip still allows the clerk or cashier to give free merchandise to a friend. However, most retail stores of any size will have the staff and the ability to observe cashiers and catch this activity.

• *Shipping* is an area of greater theft potential in the facility which is producing and shipping goods than in the retail operation. Nevertheless, in many retail situations products are delivered rather than being carried out by the customer. Here accountability procedures such as those described in Chapter 15 are essential to assure that only those products authorized by a verified sale to a recorded customer leave the storeroom or warehouse facility.

• *Accountability in the accounting department* is especially vital in the retail operation, where cash handling is ordinarily in much greater volume than in manufacturing operations. Cash, as we have seen, offers the highest level of temptation, and the primary area of security control for cash received is in the accountability procedures instituted for recording sales and receipts.

Theft through manipulation of accounting records is much the same for the retail as for the industrial operation. Accountability demands that the same person who approves payments for products cannot make the payments.

CONCLUSION

As this brief review suggests, if there is a single overriding principle in accountability, it is that there must be a separation of function or responsibility in every area of business. Only through such a separation can there be a reliable system of independent verification of purchases, verification of materials and products received, verification of inventories, verification of sales, verification of items shipped, and verification of cash and other receipts.

While no system of accountability can eliminate all possibilities of collusion designed to circumvent these verification procedures (without becoming prohibitively unwieldy, like a system of total physical security), the kind of systematic program of accountability developed and demonstrated throughout this book will make not only individual dishonesty but also collusion more susceptible to discovery and defeat.

The result will be a reinforcing of the relative honesty of the great majority of employees. By eliminating or reducing temptation, the company will not only be fulfilling its responsibility toward its employees, but it will also be reducing losses to internal theft, improving employer-employee relations, and — not incidentally — increasing profits.

And that is the bottom line.

INDEX

Index

INTERNAL THEFT: INVESTIGATION & CONTROL
An Anthology (276 pp.)
Top security professionals analyze employee dishonesty and how to control it. Includes why employees steal; undercover agents; pre-employment screening.

OFFICE & OFFICE BUILDING SECURITY
By Ed San Luis (295 pp.)
Security solutions for offices, high-rise buildings and personnel. Analyzes external and internal crimes, specific systems of defense.

CONFIDENTIAL INFORMATION SOURCES: PUBLIC & PRIVATE
By John M. Carroll (352 pp.)
Unique guide to public and private personal records. What information is on file, how it is gathered, who has access, how to identify the unknown person.

BOMB SECURITY GUIDE
By Graham Knowles (157 pp.)
Emergency program against bomb threats and letter bombs: device recognition; telephoned bomb threat procedures; evacuation, search and safety rules.

AIRPORT, AIRCRAFT & AIRLINE SECURITY
By Kenneth C. Moore (356 pp.)
Definitive study of air traffic security, from hijacking to predeparture screening; airport physical protection; fraud; air cargo problems.

HOSPITAL SECURITY
By Russell L. Colling (384 pp.)
Complete protection of people and property in health care facilities. Hospital vulnerabilities including theft of drugs, fire, disaster, internal theft.

HOTEL & MOTEL SECURITY MANAGEMENT
By Walter J. Buzby II and David Paine (256 pp.)
Loss prevention in hotel industry and protective measures for large and small hotels and motels. Includes theft, holdup, fire, fraud, restaurant and bar security, liability for injury to guests.

In addition to its hard cover books on security subjects, Security World Publishing Company publishes *Security World* and *Security Distributing & Marketing (SDM)* magazines; produces booklets and manuals on security; and sponsors the International Security Conference. Books and other materials are available from Security World Publishing Co., Inc., 2639 South La Cienega Blvd., Los Angeles, California 90034.